CASE STUDIES IN
CULTURAL ANTHROPOLOGY

GENERAL EDITORS

George and Louise Spindler

STANFORD UNIVERSITY

LIFE UNDER THE
TROPICAL CANOPY

Tradition and Change

Among the Yucatec Maya

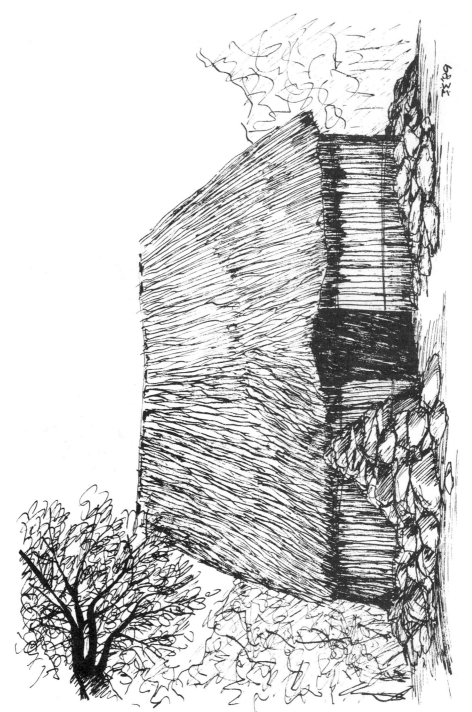

Pole-and-thatch house typical of the ancient and modern Yucatec Maya farmers.

LIFE UNDER THE TROPICAL CANOPY

Tradition and Change Among the Yucatec Maya

ELLEN R. KINTZ

State University of New York

HOLT, RINEHART AND WINSTON, INC.

Fort Worth   Chicago   San Francisco   Philadelphia
Montreal   Toronto   London   Sydney   Tokyo

Publisher: **Ted Buchholz**
Acquisitions Editor: **Chris Klein**
Project Editor: **Mark Hobbs**
Copyeditor: **Fritz Schanz**
Production Manager: **Monty Shaw**
Art and Design Supervisor: **Vicki McAlindon Horton**

Library of Congress Cataloging-in-Publication Data
Kintz, Ellen R.
  Life under the tropical canopy:
  (Case studies in cultural anthropology)
  Includes bibliographical references (p.   ).
  1. Maya—History.   2. Mayas—Social life and customs.
3. Cobá Site (Mexico)   4. Cobá (Mexico)—History
5. Human ecology—Mexico—Cobá.   6. Rain forest ecology—
Mexico—Cobá.   I. Title   II. Series.
F1435.K55   1990   972'.67   89-24534

ISBN 0-03-032592-7

Printed in the United States of America.
9 0 1 2   016   9 8 7 6 5 4 3 2 1

Holt, Rinehart and Winston, Inc.
The Dryden Press
Saunders College Publishing

To the people of Coba—the children, my peers, the elders—who taught me to experience life under the tropical canopy

Foreword

ABOUT THE SERIES

These case studies in cultural anthropology are designed to bring to students, in beginning and intermediate courses in the social sciences, insights into the richness and complexity of human life as it is lived in different ways and in different places. They are written by men and women who have lived in the societies they write about and who are professionally trained as observers and interpreters of human behavior. The authors are also teachers, and in writing their books they have kept the students who will read them foremost in their minds. It is our belief that when an understanding of ways of life very different from one's own is gained, abstractions and generalizations about social structure, cultural values, subsistence techniques, and the other universal categories of human social behavior become meaningful.

ABOUT THE AUTHOR

Ellen R. Kintz was born in New Haven, Connecticut, in 1948. She studied anthropology at the American University, Washington, D.C., and received her B.A. (1970). She received her M.A. (1976) and her Ph.D. (1978) degrees in anthropology from the State University of New York at Stony Brook. Fieldwork for her Ph.D. was carried out in Coba, Quintana Roo, Mexico, where she mapped a large residential section of the ancient Classic Maya site of Coba. This research led to her dissertation and to various publications that focused on the social organization of the ancient Maya of Coba.

In the 1980s, she returned to Coba to begin ethnographic studies. In the summers of 1980, 1982, 1983, and 1984 and in the winter of 1984–1985, she conducted research in Coba with several of her students. Studies concentrated on the history of Coba from the pre-Hispanic, Classic period to modern times. Kintz focused on the natural resources utilized by the Maya in the tropical rainforest, social organization, and Maya thought and religion.

She is currently studying ethnobotany and herbal medicine with the sole practicing *h-men* (traditional Maya priest–curer) and the *yerbateros* (herbal curers) of Coba.

Kintz has published several articles and a book on ancient Coba. She has given various papers on the social and economic organization of neighborhoods in the ancient center and on the economic organization of the modern village. She plans to return to Coba to continue her research on tradition and change under the tropical canopy.

ABOUT THIS CASE STUDY

Life Under the Tropical Canopy: Tradition and Change Among the Yucatec Maya is without precedent in the case study series. It is oriented to the natural environment "under the tropical canopy" and the uses made of this environment by the Maya for more than 13 centuries. It presents a reconstruction of Maya life during the early, middle, and late phases of its development. And it begins with a thorough description of what the author, Ellen Kintz, wanted to learn and how she went about it in the field. These seemingly disparate dimensions are woven together into a compelling analysis that is instructive as well as interesting.

Apparently, the author's training in archeology and ecology has given her a point of view that is often lacking in ethnographic studies by cultural anthropologists. It has given her the skills to experience the environment as a complex resource on which human survival is based and as a timescape that reveals evidence of prior occupation and use. It has allowed her to combine the past and the present into a continuous and interrelated whole, and each of the chapters describing and interpreting major sectors of the lowland Maya culture incorporates this point of view.

The timescape begins with the pre-Columbian period (A.D. 600–900) and continues through the Post-Classic, Colonial, and modern periods, as appropriate. One has the sense of contacting living people, real individuals, in each period. The nature of Maya culture through time emerges, with the periods as vehicles, and the continuity of the culture is demonstrated.

The 1980s has brought the greatest threat to that continuity, with its relentless population increase, its merciless exploitation of the natural environment, and its heedless advance of material technology. Even so, the Maya have survived some very bad times, and the author spares the reader no detail of these times. According to the author, Maya culture will survive into the future. The challenges of the past, the present, and the probable future faced by the lowland Maya are much like those faced by other populations in the Third World.

Currently, Ellen Kintz is studying ethnobotany and herbal medicines in the context of Maya life and the surrounding tropical forest. To do this, she has apprenticed herself to a priest–curer *(h-men)* and works with herbal curers *(yerbateros)* as well. While she is so engaged, the tropical forest from which the plants and medicines come is being destroyed. Her work may salvage some of the knowledge that will be crucial to reconstructing this system of herbal healing, thus saving invaluable resources for humankind.

This case study is an experiment in ethnography and ethnohistory. It represents a growing tradition in anthropology in which culture is regarded not as an entity, with static features and dimensions, but as a process that is enacted in contemporary space in the light of the past. This series, the *Case Studies in Cultural Anthropology,* should serve, we feel, as a vehicle for experimentation as well as a representation of the established traditions in ethnography.

GEORGE AND LOUISE SPINDLER
Series Editors
Calistoga, California

Preface

This is a book about the lowland Maya who have adapted for more than 1000 years to life on the Yucatan peninsula. Since 1975, I have worked with the Maya in the small village of Coba, located in the eastern part of the Yucatan peninsula. This book describes what the Maya have taught me about themselves, about the incredibly beautiful tropical rainforest, about the social ties that bind people to each other or shatter their relationships, and about the supernatural realm of spirits. The natural world, the social world, and the supernatural world—a world of ideas—may be separate analytical categories to us, but for the Maya, these realms blend, merge, and represent life itself under the tropical canopy.

The book is a reminder of how privileged I was to live with the Maya when their village was very small—only a hundred souls—and of how chilling it has been to see the village grow. The population has quadrupled in 10 short years and continues to grow. The village of 10 years ago was very traditional; the new village is much changed. The frontier village has been pulled into the modern world. New roads have been constructed, potable water systems have been developed, and electricity has reached the village. Still, the Maya of today retain many of their traditions, they remember many of their legends, and they continue to pass their history from the old generaion to the new.

This book presents a compilation of stories told to me by the Yucatec Maya about their life and their history and reconstructions from my own research and from that of other scholars. The names of Maya individuals have been taken from *stela* (ancient inscribed stone monuments), colonial records, historical accounts, and the living Maya. Some were or are actual persons, and some are composites. To the best of my knowledge, all represent the values, the character, and the actions of the Maya.

Ellen R. Kintz
Geneseo, New York
January 1989

Acknowledgments

The research on which this study is based has been supported by a number of public and private foundations. My initial field research in Coba (1975–1976) was supported by a National Geographic grant to Dr. William Folan and Dr. George Stuart, who hired me to assist in the production of the maps of the Ruins of Coba (Folan, Kintz, and Fletcher 1983). Dr. Folan's vision of the Maya, past and present, has profoundly influenced my own; and I thank him particularly for teaching me how to experience life in the Yucatan. I would also like to thank Dr. Stuart for his continued support of my projects on the Maya; I believe his assistance has allowed my ideas to become realities.

In 1982 and 1983, the Research Foundation of the State University of New York funded my investigations on kitchen gardens and studies with a *h-men* (traditional Maya priest–curer) and with *yerbateros* (Maya herbal curers) in Coba. The Wenner–Gren Foundation provided funding to process my field materials in the autumn of 1983. The Faculty Senate of the State University of New York at Geneseo provided funds for creating a photographic record. The Geneseo Foundation provided funding for my research and publication efforts. I am indebted to Dr. James Watson, Chairman of the Faculty Senate Committee on grants, as well as Dr. Art Hatton, Executive Director of the Geneseo Foundation, for assistance in obtaining funds. I am grateful to the National Geographic Society Committee on Exploration and Research for providing a grant (1984–1985) to enable me to continue my studies with the *h-men* and *yerbateros* and my investigations on ethnobotany.

I am greatly indebted to the directors, staff, and researchers at the Instituto Nacional de Antropologia e Historia, Merida, Yucatan, Mexico, for providing intellectual support for my projects and permitting me to make the campamento in Coba my home.

I thank my friends, colleagues, teachers, and students who have listened to 10 years of talk and ideas about the people of Coba and who have helped me in many ways. Dr. Sylvia Benton, Judy Repass, and Linda Marie Hary deserve special thanks, for without their support, the manuscript would have suffered. To Ron Pretzer and Ray Mayo, Instructional Resources, SUNY College, Geneseo, I give sincere thanks for assisting and guiding me in making the decisions on illustrations; these decisions, so close to the final stages of the manuscript, were made with great patience on their part. Denise LaDue was responsible for the final preparation of the maps in this volume, and her professional attention is greatly appreciated. I thank Warren Mianecke for preparing drawings for me and for seeing the Maya with an artist's eye. I also thank Dr. Betty Faust, who refined the manuscript with her vision of the Yucatec Maya. My appreciation is also extended to Ms. Donna Foster, who took me seriously when I asked if her press would be interested in a manuscript on the Yucatec Maya.

To my son, Nicholas Kintz Fadziewicz, thank you for listening to and enjoying the stories about the people of Coba. To my husband, Val Fadziewicz, thank you for believing I could complete this work. To Louise and George Spindler, thank you both for being sensitive editors. Perhaps, you will never realize how much it meant to me for you to enjoy reading my manuscript about the Maya.

To Melanie Stanford, Nicolas Caamal Canche and his family, Manuel May Hau and his family, Don Demetrio Pol, and Jose Isabel Cocom, thank you for helping me experience life under the tropical canopy. To the people of Coba, thank you for sharing your lives with me.

E.R.K.

Contents

List of Illustrations

LIFE UNDER THE
TROPICAL CANOPY

Tradition and Change
Among the Yucatec Maya

1/Fieldwork Among the Yucatec Maya

THE SETTING

The Yucatec Maya inhabit a great flatland plain of tropical forest in southern Mexico. The plain rose out of the sea and is mainly a limestone plate with few to no surface rivers (see Wilson 1980). The waters available to support life thread through the Yucatan peninsula beneath the surface and create a landscape of collapsed sinkholes or *cenotes,* which provide drinking water.

Since pre-Hispanic times, these cenotes have greatly influenced the placement of human settlements across the land and the organization of human social relationships. At the ancient Maya center of Dzibilchaltun, located in the northern Yucatan, a great cenote was surrounded by ancient palaces and temples. In pre-Hispanic times, the murky waters of the *Cenote Sagrado* at Chichen Itza received sacrificial victims and offerings of many kinds. The large and half-capped cenote at Valladolid, ancient Saci, remains an important gathering place for modern Maya. There are stories that the cenotes were the mouths of underground rivers, connecting ancient settlements and their peoples, and that the cenotes were the entrances to the Maya underworld.

The cenotes of Yucatan dot the peninsula, and one quickly realizes that they supported life itself in the past—as they do in the present.

The Yucatec Maya live under the tropical sun, the tropical rains, and the tropical forest. The tropics represent the most biologically rich environment on earth, with teeming vegetation and animal life. Here, in the upper stories of the rainforest, large trees can be found, such as *balche,* the bark of which the Maya use in making an intoxicating ceremonial wine, and *pom,* the resin of which is used as incense in traditional ceremonies. Also found in the upper stories is the tree called *chechem,* or "black poison-wood." The resin of this tree causes itching, blistering, and swelling; but nearby is the *chacah* trees, the juices of which serve as a cure to the rashes of the *chechem* tree (see Standley 1930). In the lower stories of the rainforest can be found *guano,* a palm with fan-shaped leaves used traditionally for house thatch, mats, or brooms. Snaking through the high rainforest is the vine *anicab,* which is used to tie house poles together and secure thatch to the roof poles of houses of the Maya. When dry, the vine will hold the house together for 50 years. This strong, pliable vine is also used by the Maya in making baskets.

The animal life in the rainforest is one of the richest in the world. Despite an increase in human settlements, hunting remains an important economic activity among the Maya, bringing venison, wild pig, and smaller animals to the Maya table. People in frontier settlements, small ranches, and campsites capture and consume monkeys, birds, and other animals.

The Yucatec Maya live within the tropical rainforest in ranchos, villages, towns, and cities. Their household patterns vary considerably from family to family and from place to place. The household is either a nuclear family consisting of husband, wife, and offspring or an extended family (most commonly three generations deep) consisting of an elderly couple, their married and unmarried offspring, and grandchildren. The organization of the family depends on the number, age, and sex of the household members. In the traditional Yucatec Maya family, social status, wealth, and political power are defined largely through the support offered by kin to achieve desired goals.

My fieldwork among the Yucatec Maya concentrated on recording traditional lifeways. However, much of what was revealed pointed to changes in life under the tropical canopy.

1975–1976

The First Days

My first experiences with the Yucatec Maya began in 1975 in the village of Coba, Quintana Roo, Mexico, where on-going research entailed survey of the Classic Maya ruins at Coba (Figure 1.1) The reconnaissance of the large archaeological site introduced me to the tropical rainforest, the living Maya, and Maya thought patterns.

The drive from Merida on the northern coast of the Yucatan to Coba on the eastern coast in Quintana Roo was a long journey in 1975. From city to village, then village to village, the population thinned out and the rainforest thickened. The highway turned to unpaved roadway. I finally reached the archaeological field camp and settled in a pole-and-thatch home. The floors were black dirt, the mosquitoes humming, the frogs croaking, and the night pitch black. That first night, I sipped hot chocolate, a traditional Yucatec Maya beverage, from a *lec,* a cup made from half a gourd. The hearth fire burned, and the smoke drifted up and out of the thatch. I hung up my hammock, tied up my mosquito net, and slipped into a cocoon to sleep.

In later years, the drive from Merida to Coba would become shorter and faster as new roads were constructed. The population in Quintana Roo would explode as more villages were established, and Coba's population would more than double. Stucco homes would be built, pole-and-thatch do-

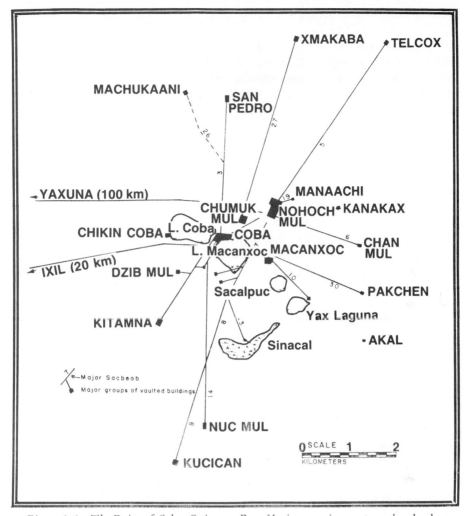

Figure 1.1. The Ruins of Coba, Quintana Roo, Mexico—major groups and sacbeob.

miciles turned into kitchens or storehouses. Native chocolate would be replaced by Nescafe and the *lec* cup by a plastic or tin mug. Hammocks would
still be used, but some people would buy mattresses and springs to sleep or
sit on in their homes.

   The first days in Coba were trying. I woke up early, walked to a nearby
structure for breakfast, and then began work—entering the rainforest to
map the ruins. I walked kilometer after kilometer to nearby ruins. The sun
was very hot, the terrain was unfamiliar, the rainforest was thick; and I was
too tired to ask questions about any of the plants. The only advice I received
was not to touch the *subin* tree, which was loaded with biting red ants, and
not to fall down, which could result in serious injury from the sharp limestone outcrops.

The First Year

The first year of work entailed a systematic survey of the archaeological ruins in the northern zone of the ancient site. As the weeks and months passed, the rainforest became more familiar. The forest at times was a high canopy *(monte alto),* a lower scrub forest *(monte bajo)*, or a few years of secondary growth *(cañada)* over an abandoned *milpa,* or cornfield. Interspersed within the forest were these *milpas,* which in the early days were surrounded by brush fences *(sop')* to keep cattle and deer out of the fields. There were clearings full of fruit trees, mostly bananas, but in relic cenotes, some *cacao* trees *(Theobroma cacao)* were grown for their chocolate beans. Also, in the forests were ranchos, homesteads isolated a few kilometers from the village itself. San Pedro was one rancho located to the north of the village of Coba. It was occupied by a man and his sons, who were rich in cattle. To the north of rancho San Pedro was another rancho, at Telcox, where a man, his wife, and their sons and daughters lived. They were known to keep wild bees, the hives housed in hollow tree trunks, in addition to the other farm activities. To the east of town was the rancho San Raphael, also occupied by a man, his wife, and their sons and daughters. To the west was another rancho, the beautiful Chac Ne.

In time, I would meet all of the families living on these ranchos, and each would provide me with a deeper understanding of Maya lifeways. Each family would work out their own strategy for adjusting to life beneath the tropical canopy. Each strategy would be distinct, and each would bring to the families successes and failures.

I traveled along the ancient Maya roads or *sacbeob*. These ancient highways built of limestone blocks and rubble were easily traveled by moonlight, and their elevation, ranging from near ground level to five meters above the forest floor, provided dry footing for travel during the rainy season. The forested areas between the ancient roads were crisscrossed by a multitude of trails leading from the village to *milpas,* hunting areas, cenotes, and orchards and to towns located in northern Yucatan. The people from Coba walked along the *sacbeob* and trails north to Chemax, Kanxoc, Tixhualatun, and Saci (Valladolid) visiting family, buying sugar, coffee, or other necessities, going to market, or seeking medical assistance.

I became dependent on social ties between myself and the people of Coba. The few stores in the village were not sufficiently stocked to provide field supplies, so corn, beans, and other foods were hauled in from Merida or the market at Carrillo Puerto more than 100 kilometers to the south. However, I did visit the three stores in Coba to buy cigarettes, matches, candles, cookies, and eggs. It was in one of the stores on a day during the first year that I began to realize how relatively wealthy the store owners were compared with other villagers and how readily they lent their money or gave credit to the people in the village. The stores were gathering places where men lounged, gossiped, drank sodas, and smoked and where women came in and out, shopped for thread and lace for the *huipiles* (traditional women's dresses; see Figure 1.2), and bought a tomato, a chile pepper, matches, or a

Figure 1.2. Woman wearing the huipil *(traditional Maya woman's dress).*

candle or two. Children also ran in and out of the stores, completed an er-
rand, bought candy or a few pieces of gum.

During this first year, the larger social world of the Maya of Coba began
to change. The papers for the Ejido de Coba, the communal land grant issued by the federal government, were received; and it was also the time
when Quintana Roo changed from being a territory to becoming a state.

Women in Coba still wore the *huipil,* with its embroidered yoke and hem (Figure 1.3) and traditional *rebozos* (shawls), but they also used bath towels as head and shoulder covers. Men had changed their daily wear to Western pants and shirts, and although they continued to wear sandals, they also bought rubber boots to wear in the rainy season. Also, men's hats were changing from the traditional straw hats to baseball caps, sometimes worn backwards.

I became involved with two families in Coba. These families supported my efforts to move through the rainforest and to unravel the social relations the people had both within and outside the village, and they helped me to become involved in understanding the supernatural world of the Yucatec Maya.

During the first year, most of my time was spent in the forest outside the village. By moving through the jungle, I began to understand the environment to which the Maya were adapting. The land around the village of Coba was covered with very limited depths of soil, either *box luum* (black soil), *chac luum* (red soil), or *k'an luum* (yellow soil), but most of it the rich, black soil favored by the *milperos* (corn farmers). The soil cover was dispersed in pockets here and there, interrupted by *butunes* (limestone outcrops), and the Maya farmers had devised an ingenious system of planting with a digging stick that allowed accurate and selective placement of seeds to take advantage of the soil distribution.

Traversing the forest, I crossed high rainforest, low rainforest, overgrown *milpas,* cut but unfired *milpas,* fired *milpas,* planted *milpas,* and other microenvironments. Although the cornfield supplied most staples, each and every environment offered special plant and animal resources. In each microenvironment, medicinal plants useful to the traditional herbalists were found. Wild animals roamed the *monte alto* and *monte bajo,* and they were found also in the *milpas.* In *cañadas* (overgrown *milpas*), fruit trees planted the previous year were found, especially the plump *put,* or papaya. Where the forest was slashed down to prepare for burning, the saplings lay over each other, forming an elevated springboard. Bounding across this mattress of saplings was dangerous, and the most common animals found here were the venomous tropical snakes.

Traversing these environments revealed varied social relations associated with each natural zone. In the *monte alto* and *monte bajo,* men hunted at night either alone or with a few of their kin or friends. Also, kin worked together to slash down trees and brush to prepare the *milpa*. If larger *milpas* were desired or could be afforded, men would hire neighbors or persons from outside the village as wage laborers to cut the field and to help plant, weed, and harvest the crops.

One night during that first year, a man came to our camp. He had slashed his foot while cutting a field, and the wound had become infected. The wound was cleaned and bound and eventually healed, but the event caused me to realize that life under the tropical canopy was full of hazards and that many of the hazards were chance events.

Figure 1.3. Child dressed in a huipil.

Another environment that I became more familiar with was the village and, on a smaller scale, the household compounds. The village was unique in that its modern settlement patterns on the south side of the lake and in the older section of the village matched fairly well the ancient Maya settlement patterns of Coba, especially the residential zones dating some 1000 years in the past. The modern settlement on the north side of the lake though, was assuming a more linear pattern, corresponding to the location of a new road. What was interesting was that one part of the village reflected the older pre-Hispanic settlement pattern, whereas another part of the village reflected a pattern quite new to the Maya living in Quintana Roo or on the frontier (Figure 1.4). This was the reality that faced the people of Coba, the struggle between tradition and change.

My attention was focused on the ancient city of Coba, but I also participated in the activities of the modern village. I became aware of the resources of the tropical forest: those resources that were wild and those that were cultivated. I began to eat the fruits of the forest and experience the foods traditionally prepared by the Maya. Their basic diet was corn, beans, and squash, but they also consumed eggs with mint, *atole* (a corn drink) with salt or sugar, candied squash, *chile del monte* (wild chile), fried pork rind, venison, *panuchos* (stuffed tortillas), and *relleno negro* (Maya stew).

During the first year, I began to enter the social world of the Maya—through the children, who are perhaps the most precious commodity that the Maya hold (Figure 1.5). Later, I would enter the world of my peers and, still later, enjoy the company of the elders. I heard about the *Chachac* ceremony (rain ceremony), participated in religious ceremonies to give thanks for a good harvest, and first heard stories about the *alux* (dwarf-tricksters).Then, the first field season came to an end, and I returned to the United States to finish my academic obligations. Over the next few years, I daydreamed about Coba. Were the people the same? Was the experience the way I recalled it to have been? In the summer of 1980, I returned to Yucatan with my husband and my one-year-old son.

1980–1985

1980: The First Time Back

When I returned to Yucatan in the summer of 1980, I was interested in studying basically two topics. One was economic production on the household level or in guildlike organizations (see Thompson 1974). Very little of the information available on the Yucatec Maya focused on this topic although much information was published on craft production and peasant economies elsewhere (see Cook and Diskin 1976; Beals 1975). The second topic I was interested in was kitchen gardens and their distribution in village, town, and city. I was interested in the kinds of gardens that were created near the household, in the nature of the diet supplementation available from these gardens, and whether the products were distributed among kin or sold.

I traveled south along the west coast of Yucatan through the towns of Muna and Ticul to Escarcega and across the base of the Yucatan Peninsula to Chetumal, Quintana Roo. From the free port of Chetumal, I traveled north along the east coast to Carrillo Puerto. From Carrillo Puerto, I trav-

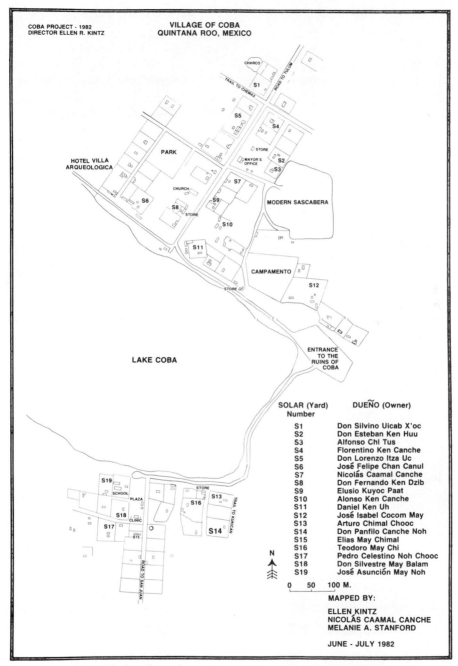

Figure 1.4. The modern village of Coba, Quintana Roo, Mexico.

Figure 1.5. Young girl in Coba.

eled north to Tulum and inland to Coba. In villages and towns throughout
the Yucatan, I observed the presence of kitchen gardens. The house compounds were surrounded by dry-laid stone walls, and within the walls were
distinctive features. Some compounds had wells and some did not, but the
vast majority of houses had kitchen gardens. Some plants were grown in

small cans or in plastic bags full of dark soil; others were grown in metal buckets full of soil. Still others were cultivated in raised or elevated garden plots. These were the *caanche,* garden plots raised to protect the plants from domestic animals. There were gardens on the ground with the soil conserved within tree trunks. Others were enclosed by stone walls, three or four rows high. More extensive gardens were enclosed in *cololche* (woven sapling fences). Within the yard area were also fruit trees such as *naranja agria* (sour orange), papaya, coconut, or banana.

In addition to the kitchen gardens and fruit trees, the houselot also contained chickens, turkeys, and pigs (Figure 1.6). Within the walls were small structures for domestic animals—chicken coops of woven saplings, small stone enclosures sometimes with *guano* (thatch) roofing, pig corrals.

During this first trip back to Yucatan, my focus was turning from the past to the present. In ancient times, the Maya produced outstanding material objects, including cotton cloth *(manta),* ceramic pieces, feathered headdresses, carved stone monuments, and musical instruments (see Adams 1970). Many of the crafts produced by the ancient Maya were perishable. Furthermore, the archaeological record to date has provided few clues as to who produced the goods and where. Were the goods produced as handicraft production in barrios of the ancient towns? Were the goods produced in guildlike organizations, in the temples of the priests, in the palaces of the Maya kings?

The large tourist, international, and food markets in Merida provided a fair idea of crafts still being produced—not only by the Yucatec Maya but also by the Indians of Mexico in general.

Figure 1.6. Domesticated turkeys strutting in Coba.

One could buy dresses from the highlands of Oaxaca, pottery from Western Mexico, leather goods from the northern desert, silver from Taxco, and more One could also buy Yucatec crafts such as hammocks, Panama hats, *rebozos* (shawls), *huipiles,* baskets, sandals, and henequen rope, mats, and bags. The Maya carpenters were selling doors and shutters for houses. One could also purchase crafts from street vendors in Merida or Valladolid (Saci). One could buy *huipil* patterns (designs for the embroidery on the yoke or hem of the dress), balsam needles for weaving a hammock, or children's toys such as tops or slingshots. For all of these goods, in 1980 the question remained, where and how were these goods produced?

My first time back to Coba revealed that several changes had occurred in the village. The population had greatly expanded, and the people of Coba no longer lived in a small frontier village. There were more opportunities inside and outside the village. The CONASUPO (Compañia Nacional de Subsistencias Populares) cooperative was opened in the town and sold goods periodically at reduced rates. There was a new tourist hotel, and it employed Cobaeños as wage laborers. Coba people were also involved in wage labor through the archaeological work at Coba and on the east coast at Tulum. Another change was the placement of an outreach clinic in Coba for treatment of various diseases. In addition, the school in Coba had been expanded.

The focus of my work during the short 1980 season at Coba involved compiling a record of all standing structures in the village and a photographic record of kitchen gardens and their variations in form. The people in the town, their families, and especially their children were also photographed. These data provided the stage for the next phase of work.

1982: Kitchen Gardens

In the summer of 1982, I returned to Coba to study kitchen gardens in detail. The research was ethno-archaeological—that is, collecting data on the modern Maya household organization to build an analog for a more detailed interpretation of the ancient Maya social organization. In addition to compiling data on kitchen gardens, I collected statistics on *milpa* harvests, on how the production of corn suffered during plagues and abnormal rainfall, and on the problems associated with the restricted sizes of the *milpa* plots. Wage labor opportunities had dramatically increased, while the base of life itself, *milpa* cultivation and harvest, had failed seven years in ten. Even so, the mixed economy of the villagers continued and *milpa* was cultivated outside the houselot to provide the staples of diet, and chickens and other domestic animals were kept within the houselot or on ranchos to supplement the diet. The number of animals kept varied considerably from family to family, as did the construction and production of kitchen gardens (Figure 1.7), arboriculture (cultivation of fruit trees), apiculture (beekeeping), and cattle holdings.

The richness of the tropical biomass is reflected in animal holdings. Fami-

Figure 1.7. Caanche *(raised kitchen garden).*

lies usually kept a few chickens and turkeys, and one family also kept ducks. Pigs were bred if the family could afford feed; cattle were kept, and savanna pasture land was planted and maintained. Some people had a horse or two or a burro to use as pack animals. Deer were caught and were sometimes kept in corrals or huts near the houses. The villagers had parrots or doves or other small wild animals as pets, and cats controlled the rat and mouse populations while dogs protected the home or announced visitors.

During this period of fieldwork, I became aware of how closely the lives of the Maya depended on their knowledge of the natural world. It was not only the cornfields that supported them. They depended also on the variety of plants grown in the forest, the condiments and supplements to the diet grown in the yard, or *solar,* and the animals kept in the walled houselot, hunted in the *milpa,* or found in the rainforest. Also, I became more aware of the substantial variation within social groupings in the village. Social success, economic success, and/or political success were promoted or prohibited by the kin ties, actual or fictive, and by ties between friends.

The size and organization of the family were significant variables in defining the wealth of families in Coba. The age of the head of the household was significant, as was the number and sex order of offspring. A family, for example, could be small and be organized as an independent nuclear family. In this case, the head of the household might be young, his wife even younger, and his offspring few. This was a difficult time for any husband and wife as they struggled to establish a home and hearth, a large and productive *milpa,* raise some chickens for eggs, and acquire other necessities such as hammocks, blankets, a table, a few chairs, and necessary clothing. Families in this category have the neatest houses because they have very few accumulated belongings.

The small nuclear family could also have a head who was quite elderly. A husband and his wife had an easy time if their grown married children lived nearby. They would be surrounded by their grandchildren, who would run errands and accompany them from place to place and who would also frequently sleep at their home.

A large nuclear family could have a relatively young head of the household and a wife and a large number of young children. There were several families of this sort in the village of Coba. When the children were all under 13 years of age and there were six or more children, the economic burden of supporting them was heavy. The fewer the number of children under 13 years of age, the less the parents had to struggle. However, when the children became old enough to assist in making *milpa* and bring income home, they rapidly became economic assets. If the bonds between child and parent were retained, the larger the number of children who reached adulthood, the more secure the elderly parents would be.

The sex order of children was also significant. If parents were going to have eight children or more, having sons first and daughters last would be to their greatest advantage. It would be the sons who would make the most significant economic contribution and at the earliest age. Daughters assisted in household chores, relieved some of the work burdens of their mother, but they contributed very little or nothing at all monetarily. The daughter was a time saver, who looked after younger children, ran a bucket of corn to the *molinero* (corn miller), and hauled buckets of water. The daughter might do laundry, water the kitchen gardens, and sew or mend clothes, but none of these activities brought in as much money as a boy could by cutting forest for *milpa,* planting or harvesting a field, working as a carpenter's assistant or as a tailor, or assisting in a store or restaurant. Sons were an economic asset because they brought in cold cash at an earlier age than daughters.

It was during this period that I was inducted into the realm of Maya thought. There was a belief system that separated the world of nature (the rainforest) from the social world (the *pueblo* or village). In the ruins of the ancient site of Coba, there were stations where the villagers burned candles and petitioned the gods to protect them when they entered the forest at night. There were spirits in the forest, there was the female *xtabai* that roamed the town, there were spirits in the *milpas,* there were the *aluxob* (dwarfs) and the *tunob* (spirits that resided in large stones). There were the important gods of rain, the *Chacob.* All of these beings conformed to an ideological system that tied the Maya to the past, regulated their actions in the present, and to some degree influenced their future.

During the summer of 1982, as part of the study of kitchen gardens and yard areas, I began to take plant samples and discovered that some of the cultivated plants and some of the wild plants from the yard were used as medicines in herbal remedies. Most of the plants were used in treating children with such ailments as fevers, diarrhea, vomiting, rashes, and stomach problems. As in most societies, women were watchful over their children and had home remedies for various childhood illnesses. Yet, in some of the house compounds, I saw an unusually wide variety of plants cultivated in general or an unusually wide variety of plants identified for use in herbal remedies.

Thus was I able to identify individuals in the village who held special knowledge concerning the plants used as herbal medicine. One man was an expert on curing snake bites, another man was skilled in treating physical ailments particular to women, several other men had general skills in treating illnesses, and there were a few women who were midwives. Several of the men in the village had been practicing *h-menob* but no longer acted as priests in carrying out traditional ceremonies. There was one practicing *h-men* for Coba, but he lived a few kilometers outside the village. During the 1982 season, I decided that a deeper understanding of the Maya world might be achieved through a study of medicinal plants. The plants would be the key to comprehend more completely the relations the Maya had to the natural world around them, to each other, and to the realm of spirits. During this season of work, I was told that every plant has its own spirit, a *sip.* I was also told that working with the plants and working as a *yerbatero or h-men* were dangerous. Without proper attention one could kill someone or one could be killed.

With the contacts made and the cooperation and assistance of the *yerbateros* and the *h-men* assured, I began to make plans to return to Coba—this time to photograph, collect, and dry-press the medicinal plants identified by the herbal curers. I would learn how to identify the plants and how they were used. I would begin to enter the world of the Maya through the natural resources of the tropical rainforest—the resources they had to protect their physical health and maintain their spiritual well being.

1983: Medicinal Plants

I returned to Coba in the summer of 1983 and began my investigations of the resources in the tropical rainforest that were used by *yerbateros* and *h-men*. The herbal remedies are akin to those reported in other traditional cultures; they are tied to the individual (not the disease) to cure the individual body and soul. The resources also include natural substances used to protect the community and to placate the spirits. Although the classification of diseases by the Yucatec Maya presents categories that are familiar, such as aches and pains, asthma, bowel complaints, chills and fevers, fainting, mouth/tongue/nose complaints, and insanity, these are only one level of the diagnoses, treatments, and cures practiced by the Maya curers.

Yucatec Maya herbal curers have been monitoring the physical and mental health of the villagers for a very long time. It is a task that is very amenable to small-scale community life. The herbal curers are in contact with their wards on a daily basis. Traversing the town for small purchases in the stores or visiting house-to-house are patterns characteristic of Maya village life. Movements to and from the *milpas* or orchard plots, traveling into the forest to collect honey or other products, watering cattle, hunting—these are activities that encourage a high measure of social interaction and, for the herbal curer or the Maya priest, provide many opportunities to monitor the welfare of the village members.

A review of the medicinal plants used by the modern Maya in traditional curing reveals the segmental nature of, but complementary relationship among, their natural, social, and cosmic environments. Plants are used in combination to treat individual ailments, body and soul. Beyond the herbal remedies used to cure physical ailments, plants are used to prevent or cure other classes of infirmity that are not as familiar to the Western mind. In various combinations, they are used to treat *mal ojo* (evil eye), *mal viento* (evil winds that strike one and cause debilitation), and the illnesses caused by *ikims* (children with double whirls of hair on their heads, double teeth, and whirls of hair on their backs who are thought to "eat" or kill their younger siblings who are not *ikims;* see Figure 1.8). *Mal ojo* is said to cause severe diarrhea in infants, dehydration, and death; *mal viento* is said to cause headache, heartache, general debilitation, and death in adults. The people say that these illnesses cannot be cured by the Western medical professional, rather these illnesses can be cured only by a Maya *h-men*.

The social environment of the family and its holdings is protected by a variety of rituals that incorporate medicinal plants. The *Lolcatali* was a ritual for protecting the houselot or village from evil spirits; *Los Corrales,* for protecting cattle and corrals; *U-hanli-col,* for protecting the *milpa* and the fam-

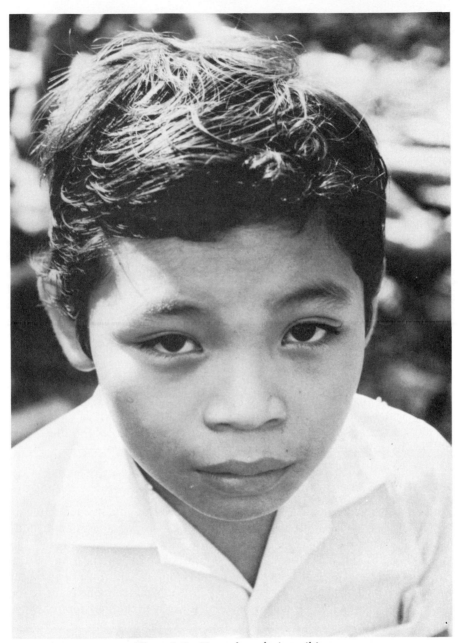

Figure 1.8. Young boy who is an ikim.

ily that worked it; *U-hanli-cab,* for protecting wild bees and the family that
had them.

The cosmic realm was propitiated by rituals that also used medicinal
plants. These were rituals to call the Rain Gods, the *Chacob,* to propitiate
the *alux* and the *tun,* spirits of the forest, and so on.

I collected information on over 300 disease categories compiled by Ralph Roys (1931) from ethnohistorical documents and hundreds of medicinal plant samples recorded by Alfredo Barrera Marin, Alfredo Barrera Vazquez, and Rosa Maria Lopez Franco (1976). I traversed segments of the natural and social environment and searched for plants in houselots, along trails, in cultivated and abandoned *milpas,* in the *monte bajo* and *monte alto* as well as in *acalche* (wooded swamps) and along the shores of lakes. A review of the literature on archaeological sites of the Classic and post-Classic Maya revealed pictorial representations of plants and animals on murals, carved monuments, and tomb covers. Review of the ethnohistoric literature provided additional references to plants and animals and their uses as medicinal substances as well as for clothing, building materials, and in various ceremonies.

The array of plants provided the key to enter the natural world of the Maya and provided considerable insight into social action and cosmic forces. As I became more familiar with the array of plants and natural resources used by the Maya, it became apparent that some individuals were more astute in manipulating the resources than were others. Life under the tropical canopy was much more than *milpa* cultivation, more than raising chickens and other domestic fowl, and more than cultivating kitchen gardens. Life was a social phenomena that was interrelated with natural and cosmic forces, and the individuals most astute at coordinating natural forces, social action, and cosmic beings were the *yerbateros* and *h-menob.* These individuals held the most complex and complete corpus of data concerning Maya social and cultural traditions. I initiated a research strategy to work more closely with these individuals to understand the Yucatec Maya culture and society. It was time to begin to work with the elders who were the keepers of knowledge concerning the core of Maya culture.

Yerbateros and *H-menob*

One of the major goals of ethnographic fieldwork and anthropology is to obtain a holistic view of culture. Ten years of fieldwork and academic study of the Yucatec Maya represented a slow but progressive move toward this goal. The outsider enters the natural and cultural environment of the Yucatan as a child, drowning in a sea of green—swimming in and swamped by the canopy, entangled in the vines, and barely able to step from one place to another. Only after nearly 10 years of walking literally in the footsteps of Maya guides did I begin to move through the jungle with a clearer understanding of the beauty that surrounded me. I can remember one particularly difficult outing in 1976 when I visited the rancho of Demetrio Pol, to the west of Coba village at Chac Ne (Figure 1.9). I went to the rancho to map the area and, intrigued by the multitude of ancient mines *(sascaberas)* around the isolated pole-and-thatch structures, I entered the forest only to become hopelessly lost. Without a guide, my sense of distinction between human living space and the natural world eroded. No compass to guide me, no water, and no machete to defend me, the forest became overwhelming, frightening, and

Figure 1.9. Demetrio Pol, practicing h-men, *at his rancho, Chac Ne.*

threatening. This fear resided within me the first time I met Demetrio Pol. I mapped his *rancho* although he spoke very limited Spanish and I spoke no Yucatec Maya. I was impressed by the beauty of the place. The family had carved a home out of the rainforest, and the structures and ancillary buildings were set out in a form similar to house compounds I had mapped in the

Ruins of Coba dating back some 1000 years. Later, I would learn more about the man, his family, and their history. Demetrio Pol was the sole practicing *h-men* living in Coba.

In 1982, I returned to visit Demetrio Pol at Chac Ne to collect census data and information on his kitchen gardens and orchards. The orchard information amazed him—and me—for over the years he had cultivated more than 200 trees around his domicile. In 1983, I walked again to Chac Ne to meet with Don Demetrio. I went to ask him to teach me about the medicinal plants used by the Maya curers and to learn how they were used. He explained the dangers associated with manipulating the plants. "Not everyone is capable of working with the plants. You need to concentrate on them to the exclusion of all. They can harm you; you can kill someone. You need to go through a ceremony to protect yourself. There are spirits associated with them. But I will teach you." In this way I took an apprenticeship with this Maya *h-men*. With him my understanding of the nature, human interaction, and spirit world known to the Maya began and a holistic view of the Yucatec Maya culture would emerge. Walking to Chac Ne in the summer of 1984, following the footsteps of my assistant, we again became lost in the tangle of vegetation. But as we moved through the forest, I realized that we needed just to push on; shortly, we would reach Chac Ne and Demetrio Pol and begin to unravel the mystery of the Maya. The trips to Chac Ne were trips back in time. The village of Coba was rapidly changing, rapidly growing, and entering a new era; yet traversing the forest—entering deeper and deeper—to the isolated rancho was a trail deeper and deeper into the traditional world of the Maya.

In the summer of 1984, Demetrio Pol was asked to hold a *Chachac* rain ceremony in a village to the south of Coba. After the ceremony, I sat in his kitchen and ate *nohua* (large tortillas) with *pepita* and gravy and drank black coffee with sugar. The traditional ceremonies to call the Rain Gods, protect the pueblo or the household, and protect the cattle and corral were becoming infrequent. The social gatherings associated with these ceremonies and the association and cooperation among villagers were eroding. The new religions focused more on the individual than on the group, and the *ejido* and *municipio* politics were eclipsing the old traditional order. Don Demetrio Pol taught me to see the relationships between the natural world, the social world, and the cosmic world. I would also see more clearly that the traditions were rapidly changing (For a photograph of the author, see Figure 1.10.)

In 1983 when I returned to collect medicinal plants in Coba, I began to work with Jose Isabel Cocom. He was a practicing *yerbatero* and had been trained as a *h-men* although he had abandoned this work. Toward the end of our summer 1983 season, I asked him if he would help me collect medicinal plants and if he would teach me how they were used. As I walked with Jose Isabel, the natural world became more familiar. He trained me to see the amazing variety of plants and to look in hidden places, cross trails, and to seek the smallest plants and recognize the uses of the largest trees. He ex-

Figure 1.10. Photograph of the author.

plained that plants had "seconds" *(segundos)* so that if one plant was not available in a season, another could be used. He remembered where rare plants were located and showed me which plants were used for love potions by a man to capture the love of his life and which were used by a woman to capture the attention of a young man. Jose Isabel was elderly, maybe 55 years old, and had grown children who had married and had their own children. Working with him introduced me to the close social ties between the elders and their grandchildren. Whether walking in the forest or sitting in his house, I enjoyed the close relationship he had with his young grandson. The child sat close by, listening to us work; and when our backs ached and we needed a break, we would watch the child, play with him, or rest a bit. These were some of the best times in Coba, truly participating in family life.

In the summer of 1984, I returned to Coba with my husband and my four-year-old son. As I continued my work with Jose Isabel Cocom, my son played with his grandson and the other children of Coba. I recorded stories about Maya cosmological forces and the social actions of the Maya and continued to collect plants. In the winter of 1984–1985, I returned to Coba to continue work with Jose Isabel Cocom and Don Demetrio Pol. During these sessions of fieldwork, I continued to collect information on kinship ties and was invited to attend two weddings. I worked with the Maya, constructed kitchen gardens, and collected information on arboriculture and beekeeping. Opportunities for wage labor were expanding for the Maya, more stores and restaurants were opening, and communal projects were being carried on, including an extensive reforestation program and a fish cooperative (Figure 1.11). People were working on a seasonal basis on the coast, and the corn harvests were slim. As I became a chronicler of history, the society and culture were changing. I began to look toward the future. What was Coba to become?

Figure 1.11. Fish cooperative at Lake Coba. The cooperative failed when the nets ripped and the fish escaped.

2/Life Under the Tropical Canopy

THE NATURAL ENVIRONMENT

From the air, the east coast of the Yucatan peninsula appears to be a flat plain covered with a dense canopy of trees. It is interspersed with open areas marking slash-and-burn agricultural fields and small towns, villages, and isolated homesteads of the Yucatec Maya. The geological base is limestone, a karst topography with pockets of soil, granular limestone deposits *(sascaberas),* and limestone sinkholes *(cenotes).* Running northeast to southwest is a fault line that opens in the area of Coba in a series of lakes including Lake Coba, Lake Macanxoc, and other minor water resources. Around the Coba lakes, populations gathered in pre-Hispanic times in periodic concentrations, building temples, palaces, ballcourts, and ordinary house compounds. In more recent times, seasonal *chiclero* camps along the lake shores were occupied by populations moving in from the northern Yucatan. About 40 years ago, the village of Coba was established by five men and their families. The Ejido de Coba, communally held agricultural land, was established in 1975.

The natural resources in the area permitted success in hunting, encouraged farming, and allowed the creation of savanna (grasslands) to feed cattle herds. The useful geological resources in the area were mainly limestone blocks cut in pre-Hispanic times for building materials. The limestone blocks created temples for ceremony, palace structures housing the elite, and block construction in rectangular forms filled with rubble elevating the house mounds of the less prestigious pre-Hispanic populations concentrated around the Coba lake zone. Granular limestone pockets were extensively mined, provided a stucco cement to plaster ancient buildings, and served as the base for frescos such as those that face Las Pinturas or El Cuartel in the Ruins of Coba (Folan, Kintz, and Fletcher 1983). The limestone blocks and rubble were also used to build extensive roads or *sacbeob* that has made the Ruins of Coba famous in the archaeological literature on the ancient Maya. These roads radiate from the core of the ancient city, and one roadway extends to the west 100 kilometers into the modern state of Yucatan. Whether the roads were traveled by the elite in ceremonial processions or by traders moving goods from the eastern portions of the peninsula to the drier western sectors is still debated, but the roads connected the prehistoric peoples of the Coba region to populations in other polities. This economic, social, and ideological connection has continued from ancient times to the present.

The Coba geological base is also characterized by a complex distribution of soil types classified by the Maya and related to the fertility of the soil categories. Near the Coba lakes, rich deposits of fertile black soils *(box luum)* are found. Although pocketed and interrupted by limestone outcrops, the soil has eroded into relic cenotes and into the bottoms of ancient open *sascab* mines for thousands of years. Ringing the Coba lakes is an enormous *sascab* mine that was excavated to provide the plaster, rubble, and limestone blocks for the creation of the extraordinary stone ruins found around the lakes. The modern village of Coba is seated on and among these ancient ruins, and the excavated mines provide pockets of *box luum* used for cultivation of modern orchards and kitchen gardens. The lands used by the modern Maya for agricultural production ring the village. Nearly all of the modern agricultural land is rich, black soil with the exception of lands a few kilometers to the north, south, east, and west where less fertile red soils *(chac luum)* are found. Interspersed with these major soil categories are pockets of yellow soil *(k'an luum)*. Each of these soils produces agricultural products with different success, and the Maya plant accordingly, choosing seeds or cuttings that are adapted to each soil's fertility and ability to retain water. Although the black soil is the most fertile, favored and able to hold water the longest, various cultivated species thrive in the other soil categories. The most noticeable characteristic of the terrain is minor slopes that encourage soil erosion, expose bedrock, and give the terrain a spotty or patchy distribution of soils useful for planting crops or orchards.

Coba is situated in the east-central Yucatan peninsula, an area of Tropical Wet and Dry climate (Koeppen Aw classification), and the vegetation is classified as Semi-Evergreen Seasonal Forest (Vivo Escoto 1964). The tropical rains come to Coba in May, are heaviest in July and August, and decrease by October. November to May marks the dry season. It is in May or June that agricultural fields are planted, and the corn harvests are reaped in the early fall. From November to May during the dry season, the rainforest is cut down and dried in preparation for another agricultural cycle. During the dry season, the forest sheds some of its leaves, and the landscape takes on a burned appearance under the strong tropical sun. Mean annual rainfall averages 1500 mm (Wilson 1980, p. 24), but there is considerable variation from year to year and area to area. The year-to-year variation is troublesome to the agricultural activities, and cycles of rainfall are a significant preoccupation of the Maya farmer. If the rains are early, the firing of fields is unsuccessful. If the rains are tardy, the planted seeds fail to germinate.

The instability of the rainfall pattern greatly influences harvest yields and has acted to encourage social cooperation among families related by kin ties or bonds of friendship (Folan, Kintz, and Fletcher 1983). Larger extended families act to offset the variation in yields by cutting large *milpa* plots in different local areas. Success in *milpa* harvests permits accumulation of dry corn supplies, which can be stored for up to three years. These stores may feed the families that collected the corn or may be sold to less successful neighbors. Large harvests also permit investment in other ventures—either in traditional ways such as increasing one's holdings of chickens, turkeys, pigs, cattle, beehives, or fruit trees, or in entrepreneurial activities such as opening a small store or restaurant. Every family in Coba agrees that the route to economic success is through the cultivation of large *milpa* plots. Every Coba family that is comparatively wealthy was originally successful in agricultural activities.

The rainforest in the Coba area is Semi-Evergreen Seasonal Forest and mostly a two-story seasonal canopy (Wilson 1980). The tropical rainforest generally is three stories, but in some climax forest areas, five stories of woody plants form a closed canopy and thus screen sunlight from the forest floor. The tallest trees found near Coba are *ramon,* found clustered in the center of the Ruins of Coba, as isolated trunks dispersed around some households, and growing sporadically in the outlying *ejido* zone. *Ramon* leaves are used by the modern Cobaeños for cattle feed. *Alamo* is another large tree found in the area and is used in making paper. Cedar is becoming a rare find in the Coba region, but it is still favored to make small seats, doors, and window shutters by the Maya. *Quiebrahacha,* a small hardwood tree (only 10 meters tall) and *Tancazche,* another small tree, are found in the *monte alto* (high rainforest) around Coba. The root cover on this the *Tancazche* is masticated for treatment of toothaches, which results in a numbing of the pain. These trees are all characteristic of *monte alto.* When the modern village was first occupied as a frontier settlement, the area of high rainforest was extensive. During the last 40 years with in-migration and population explosion in the area, the town and surrounding *ejido* zone have been reduced to *monte bajo* (low rainforest), *cañada* (scrub growing in abandoned *milpa* plots), and *milpa* fields.

Under the closed canopy of climax forest, the floor is mainly free of vegetation because of the lack of sunlight. This high rainforest is favored by *milperos* (corn farmers) for slash-and-burn agriculture. The character of the Semi-Evergreen Seasonal Forest in climax permits leaf accumulation and mulching of the thin tropical soils. Furthermore, the closed canopy breaks the force of the tropical rains, reducing the leaching of nutrients from the thin soils. Without the protection of upper-story vegetation, the soils are drained of their nutrients by torrential rains (leached) or baked to hardpan by the tropical sun (lateritic soil formation). The agriculturalists of Coba are aware of these problems in farming the land and state that 50 years of agricultural rest are necessary for the climax forest to regenerate. Unfortunately, population pressure on limited available land resources prohibit a fallow period of this length. Farmers do let the forest regenerate over their abandoned *milpas,* but the fallow period can be as short as five years, which would permit the regeneration of the *monte bajo* only.

In the low rainforest, which covers most land around the modern village of Coba, useful and valued forest species are found. The resin-bearing *pom* and the wine-producing *balche,* valued by the ancient Maya, are used re-

spectively by the modern Maya for making incense and a ceremonial beverage (Figure 2.1). *Zapote* is also found in Coba forests, and in the past it was
found in considerable numbers. This tree is cut for *chicle* sap, and in the recent past before the modern village was settled, *chiclero* camps were located

Figure 2.1. The bark from the balche *tree, and other ingredients, produce wine for traditional
ceremonies.*

near the center of the Ruins of Coba. There is no *chiclero* activity in Coba now, but *zapotes* are found in great numbers to the east of the Coba *ejido;* and these are currently producing sap, which is transferred to Tulum on the east coast and then south to Carrillo Puerto to be processed through a *chiclero* cooperative. Another economically important resource found in the *monte bajo* is *guano*. It is said to be left standing when ground is cleared and can attain heights of 24 meters, towering over *milpas,* and is also found growing closer to the forest floor. The fan-shaped leaves of *guano* are used for thatch in roofing (Standley 1930, p. 219).

An additonal microenvironmental niche found in the Coba area is the *acalche* or wooded swamp. These swamps are covered with a shallow sheet of water during the rainy season, and the water evaporates during the dry season. Along the sides of *acalche* in Coba, *chacmolche* is found. This small, spiny tree produces scarlet seeds that are poisonous (Standley 1930, p. 295). *Bilimcoc* is also found along the edge of the *acalches*. This plant is used in a medical remedy for *coc* (asthma) (Roys 1931; Jose Isabel Cocom, personal communication).

The village of Coba is located north and south of Lake Coba, and the natural plant resources around the lake are also useful to the Maya. *Naab,* the water lily, which figures prominently in ancient Maya iconography, floats along the lake shore. *Chapak* is also found here. This common weed can be used to treat skin diseases (Standley 1930; Roys 1931; Jose Isabel Cocom, personal communication). Reeds and grasses are also located in this microenvironment.

Cañadas (abandoned overgrown *milpas*) offer another environment that presents a different plant community. Although an abandoned *milpa* appears to be an overgrown weed patch, it does have important plant species. *Balsamito* is found here and is used by the *yerbateros* to treat dysentery (Jose Isabel Cocom, personal communication). *Ximche* (see Barrera Marin, Barrera Vazquez, and Lopez Franco 1976, p. 168 and plate 4) is also found and used by the Maya to cover the arches over the ceremonial table in the *Chachac* rain ceremony. The *ximche* has seeds the color of maize and when these ripen, they are a signal to the Rain Gods to bring rain so that the maize can grow (Jose Isabel Cocom, personal communication). A *cañada* also may have fruit trees planted by the farmer in the previous year, of which *put* (papaya) is one.

The *milpa* plot also has a distinct series of plant species (Figure 2.2). The most prevalent plant species in *milpa* fields are maize, beans, and squash. Jicama (Standley 1930) is also cultivated in the *milpas,* and the roots of this plant are eaten as a dietary supplement or as a staple. The cultivated fields of the Maya are central to their lives and are the focus of considerable conversation. The natural forces that affect planting and harvest, the social relations that are acted out in the village, and Maya ideological precepts revolve around making *milpa*. The natural setting of the *milpa* reflects its temporary existence within the tropical rainforest. It is cut out of the jungle, but one day, it will transform back into rainforest. In its special form, the cultivated

Figure 2.2. Milpa *located to the west of the village of Coba.*

field is much like the jungle, recreated in miniature. The same natural forces that attack the forest rain and shine on the cultivated field. Animals wander into the field and feed off its products, much to the distress of the inattentive Maya farmer. These forest fauna that enter the field are also the animals that, with luck, the Maya may take for their tables at home or for ceremonial feasts. The attentive Maya make visits to the *milpas* at night, hang their hammocks up in treetops, and wait for feeding deer or wild pig. The field is rich in cultivated species, similar to the tropical forest with an exuberance of wild species. Corn, beans, and squash are not the only species cultivated; others include varieties of chile peppers, root crops, and various fruit trees. Part of the agricultural cycle entails weeding the field, and some of the weeds are valued species used in medicinal remedies.

Plants also thrive along trails and walkways within the village. Some of these are also valued for medicinal uses or as supplemental condiments. In Coba, for example, we located a large wild *chile del monte* bush (Barrera Marin, Barrera Vazquez, and Lopez Franco 1976, p. 216). This "chile of the forest," with pods the size of a small fingernail (1 cm long), is useful when cultivated chile is unavailable or too expensive. The tiny fruit burns the tongue.

Another man-made environment is the yard or *solar*. This enclosed space is another miniature replica of the natural forest. The diversified ecological resources found in the forest and replicated in *milpa* plots are artificially duplicated again in the yard area in kitchen gardens. According to Anderson (1952), in San Pedro Tlaquepaque in western Mexico, although the yard areas look like dump heaps with a few trees, they in fact contain vegetable gardens, orchard areas, medicinal plants, compost heaps, areas for protecting animals and beehives, and flower gardens for bee feeding.

The yard areas of tropical horticulturalists have not been neglected by ethnographers in Mesoamerica. Kitchen gardens have been reported on in western Mexico (West 1948; Brand 1951), in the Gulf Coast Totonac area (Kelly and Palerm 1952), in the Guatemala highlands (Wisdom 1940; McBride 1947) and in Yucatan (Smith and Cameron 1977; Redfield and Villa Rojas 1934; Lundell 1937). Joyce Marcus (1982) has noted that the Motul dictionary gives the Yucatec Maya term *chol pakal* for "garden," and *putz luum* for "dry soil without stones." The stoneless soil may have been transported into the soil-deficient *solar* to fill garden plots. Marcus (1982, p. 268) also suggests that a 20- by 20-meter garden plot would have had three to 10 vegetable crops. This is the size and form of many kitchen gardens in the yard areas of Coba. The kitchen gardens of the modern Yucatec Maya illustrate sophisticated intercropping regimens that attempt to adapt to rainforest environmental restraints (lateritic and leaching problems).

For the Maya living under the tropical canopy, adaptation to various segments of the natural environment is a necessity. From the air, life seems to respond to the possibilities and limits of manipulating the tropical canopy. From the ground, adaptation is made to the limestone karstic topography. By moving through the natural microenvironmental zones, one can gain a sense of the diverse products of the rainforest, natural resources, and artificially created resources. The segments of the natural environment include the *monte alto*, which is especially productive for hunting; the *monte bajo*, which also holds economically important game resources; the *cañadas*, with orchard products; the *milpas,* with corn, beans, squash, and other seed and root plants; the trails, with ceremonial and economically important species; and the *solares,* with more artificial cultivation and space for important domesticated animals. All segments also provide plant and animal species used as medicinal substances by *yerbateros* and *h-men.*

THE SOCIAL ENVIRONMENT

The people of Coba not only adapt to the natural world around them but also participate in a social world. The most immediate social network that influences action is the nuclear or extended family found within the walled houselot compound. The nuclear family—a man, his wife, and offspring—is the smallest social unit that is responsible for the physical health and well being of its members (Figure 2.3). The family teaches Maya cultural values, begins the socialization of individuals, and rewards proper social behavior. The extended family, most commonly three generations deep, brings the wisdom of elders, the energy of younger married couples, and the responsibility of childrearing together in a single economic unit.

Variation in family organization is considerable among the families in the village of Coba and may account for the success or distress of any individual family group. Nuclear families range in size from newlywed couples with few offspring and limited economic resources to older married couples with many offspring and many material resources. Extended families vary in size and in level of economic cooperation. In all families, the relationships between husband and wife are symbiotic. The husband contributes the bulk of economic resources, especially the bulk of food staples. The wife supplements family income in various ways and is also responsible for running the household from day to day and, most importantly, cooking meals for the entire family. The husband works in the *milpa* and provides wild game while the wife cares for the kitchen gardens and feeds and tends the chickens, turkeys, and pigs that the family has accumulated. The work load on the husband and wife is heavy.

Although considerable socializing occurs day to day, it is usually coincidental with other tasks. Women gossip in the morning on their way to the *molinero* (corn miller) and may continue to gossip when hauling water out of communal wells. Women exchange information when they visit stores to buy candles, laundry soap, a few eggs, or chile peppers. People yell news over house compound walls as they walk through town on errands. The work load of women is continuous. They are responsible for feeding their families in the morning—making the cooking fire, boiling water for their husband's coffee, and preparing food to be taken by him to the *milpa.* The women soak their corn, rinse it, and grind it into *masa* (corn dough) to make a mountain of tortillas that are consumed daily as a staple by family members. Beans are boiled, and the fire burns all day within three hearth stones covered by a metal *comal* (griddle). Although food preparation is a primary occupation of women, they also sweep their houses, do their family's laun-

Figure 2.3. Nuclear family of Florentino Cen, his wife, and their children.

dry, feed their chickens, turkeys, and pigs, and tend to their kitchen gardens. They must dress the younger children, feed them, and bathe them
every day. Women may sew and embroider *huipiles* (traditional Maya
women's dresses), and they mend their family's clothes.

The most extensive work that men perform is *milpa* agriculture, and it is the focus of their lives. Men cut the forest down with axes and machetes, fire their fields, and plant their crops. They visit their *milpas* mostly every day, every three days at a minimum, and they weed their fields and harvest the crops. The corn may be stored in *nainales* (corn cribs) in the *milpa*, and the men haul sacks of dry ears of corn back to their homes to be processed for consumption. Men also carry other products home from the *milpa*, including beans, squash, jicama, *macal*, and other minor products. They may also maintain orchards outside the village, the fruits of which are vitamin rich and are collected to enhance the main diet of corn, beans, and squash.

Some men in Coba also work on the local reforestation cooperative (COPLAMAR). They receive wages for excavating and transporting soil, building raised gardens, watering and monitoring the seedling beds, transporting saplings, and working in the reforestation areas. In Coba, men have an opportunity for wage labor in the tourist hotel established in the late 1970s. They can work as watchmen, janitors, waiters, cooks, or mechanics. Wage labor opportunities are also available for men on the east coast where tourist development is booming. Cobaeños have been hired as archaeological crew members in the Ruins of Coba, on the east coast at Tulum, and in Campeche at Calakmul.

The movements of the men may extend away from the village when they are wage laborers, but the women remain within the boundaries of home and local village. Children within the family assist with chores that are mainly sex specific. Young girls tend their younger siblings, learn to make tortillas, do laundry, feed domestic animals, and run errands, replicating their mother's work and stay close to the hearth. Young boys have more freedom to move through the village and beyond to assist their fathers in the *milpas* and to learn to hunt, and by adolescence, they are working to bring cash in to the family (Figure 2.4). Young boys may collect firewood and sell it, run errands for a tip, or work in the small restaurants in town.

The social group most influential on the individual, young or old, is the family. The family supplies economic resources, provides individuals with a social position, offers assistance in work requirements, and gives psychological support. It is the primary teaching agency although a local primary school is attended by most children in Coba.

A larger social group is the village itself, where kinsmen and friends interact in a variety of places. Visiting from household to household is a common practice in Coba. Interaction among village members is face to face and a daily occurrence. When I first began to participate in Maya life and visited women during the day, we relaxed in hammocks, joked, sang, and played with the children. I remember thinking how little work was done by my women friends during these periods. Later, as I became more than a guest, I realized how polite the Maya were in treating formal visitors. As my relationships with the women became more informal, I began to participate in their work cycle. Children needed to be washed, dressed, and have their hair combed. There were tortillas to be made, animals to be fed, and garden areas to be tended. Close women friends visit and work together. I have sewn

Figure 2.4. Young boy with a tumpline hauling water.

seams with the women, made tortillas, and constructed garden plots. The
work is exhausting but exhilarating, for friendship has extraordinary social
and economic benefits. The socializing between families makes everyone's
economic resources public knowledge, and this encourages exchange. The

cooperation between families permits an input of energy beyond that available to a single household, a man, or his wife; and the cooperation is reciprocal although not necessarily parallel. Women who have helped create a garden plot in their neighbor's yard may receive a bunch of herbs or a load of firewood in exchange for their assistance.

There are a few stores in Coba where entrepreneurial members of the village have accumulated sufficient resources to supply their neighbors with necessary goods. In 1975 and 1976, the stores were one room, pole-and-thatch structures with limited goods. There were three stores in Coba, all operated by elders, and although they all had soft drinks, not a single store had cold drinks. The stores had chewing gum, graham crackers, soda crackers, some canned vegetables, salt, sugar, cigarettes, matches, very thin candles, thread and cloth for *huipiles,* and a limited number of additional items. Corn and beans were sold, and sometimes eggs were available. Limited supplies of medicine were also available. In the 1980s, the stores were larger and had storage rooms attached to the side or rear. All of the stores had cold colas or other soft drinks, and there were more items for sale. One could buy notebooks, pens, toiler paper, Cloralex bleach, a variety of soaps, flashlights, replacement bulbs and batteries, large tins of chocolate chip cookies, blankets, hammocks, fresh vegetables, fruit, several types of potato chips, Twinkies, and other items. If the store didn't have a particular item, it could be ordered from Valladolid and delivered in a short time. Villagers could receive credit from the store owners as they could in the past. In 1975 and 1976, the stores were dark during the day, and at night, they were lit by candles. In the 1980s, each store had a generator, and electric light bulbs swung from the ceiling.

In 1975, the village women processed their corn by pressing it through a hand grinder *(molino).* By the 1980s, there were two *molineros* (corn millers) with gas-run motorized corn grinders in the village. In one house there was a gigantic machine to make tortillas, but I never saw it run and the women continued to make tortillas by hand and cook them over the *comal.* Coba also had a pool hall where men could gather in the evenings to play billiards, gossip, and drink beer. In 1975 and 1976, there was not a single restaurant in the village. By the 1980s, four restaurants had been built, although one had failed, and in addition, the tourist hotel in Coba offered breakfast, lunch, and dinner but at exorbitant prices. The tourist hotel also opened a boutique, and there were two *artesanias,* or craft stores, in the village run by local families serving the tourists who came to visit the Ruins of Coba.

Coba had a small medical clinic that served the village people and drew clients from surrounding isolated ranchos and frontier communities to the north, south, and east. There was a primary school located in the town as well. In 1982, the people of Coba cleared land, and the state government assisted in creating a plaza where dances were held occasionally. These sections of the town were areas where people worked and relaxed.

The people of Coba also participated in more far-flung social networks. They interacted with villages and *ejidos* in the areas beyond the boundaries of the village and Coba *ejido*. Relations with other villages and *ejidos* were tied to kinship or friendship. Some inhabitants of Coba migrated out to form new settlements. Sons and daughters married out of the village, and some families abandoned the village to settle on isolated ranchos. The resident population of Coba was fluid; people moved out of the village to take advantage of economic opportunities that seemed more favorable, or people moved back to the village when politics in another area were unstable.

Social relations in Coba extended along the route from Coba to Tulum on the east coast. Much of this land had been national forest in 1975 and 1976, but beginning in the 1980s, it was occupied by established villages and *ejido* lands. As the land around the village of Coba became used and converted to *monte bajo,* some families moved east into the *monte alto* to live and farm. Most of the land along the road has now been settled and claimed, and the people in this string of villages and ranchos maintain social ties to each other.

The people of Coba also maintain social ties to the state of Yucatan. Forty years ago when the village of Coba was settled, families that first came to the area migrated in from small towns south of Valladolid. Ties with relatives living in Kanxoc, Tixhualatun, and Chemax were still maintained, and the people of Coba walked or traveled by horse or burro along trails and *sacbeob* to visit relatives in Yucatan. People still travel to these towns, but bus lines are used now, making the trip much easier.

Valladolid to the northwest and Carrillo Puerto to the south were used by the Cobaeños for medical services before there was a village clinic, and some families continue to use doctors in these areas when need arises. The markets and stores in Valladolid were used by villagers in the mid-1970s when few goods were sold in Coba. Now, most items can be obtained in Coba although the cost of an item may be higher in the village than in the city.

The villagers are also aware of larger social settings. They have traveled and worked up and down the east coast of Quintana Roo and are familiar with villages and towns in the state of Yucatan. Some of the men of Coba have traveled to Campeche and have worked at the archaeological site of Calakmul. The Coba people are aware of the political power centered in Mexico City. The radios in the village broadcast news about the United States, and Castro has come from Cuba to visit Tulum, and some of the Cobaeños went to hear him speak. The French Club Mediterranean has built a Villa Arquelogica in the village to house and feed wealthy tourists.

Although the world of the Yucatec Maya continues to be focused on home and hearth, the larger world has had an impact on village life in many ways. The collapse of the international oil market has almost devastated Mexico, and the federal funds for many economic projects in the outback have had to be cut. Government funding for the COPLAMAR reforestation project has been cut, limiting the wage labor opportunities for the people of Coba. Inflation in Mexico has driven up the prices of maize and beans, and all purchased items have become more expensive, sometimes increasing in price from week to week. The growing tourist industry on the east coast of the Yucatan peninsula has opened wage labor opportunities for villagers but has caused some disruption in *ejido* organization. The social patterns of the Maya are embedded in traditions that reach back in time, but at the same time, the world of the Maya is undergoing significant change and their life-style is evolving. One wonders what kinds of social networks will operate in the future.

THE SUPERNATURAL ENVIRONMENT

The world of the Yucatec Maya is populated with supernatural beings and forces. Analysis of the supernatural world provides information defining the relationship of the Maya to the natural world and to each other. As in all societies, there exist among the Yucatec Maya "keepers of knowledge." These are Maya priest-curers, the *h-menob*. These individuals are trained to carry out traditional ceremonies and to communicate with supernatural be-ings and forces. They monitor the welfare of individuals and related eco-nomic resources as well as the welfare of larger social groups. They petition the supernatural forces to act in aid of Maya society and also to cure individ-uals stricken by supernatural illnesses. The *h-menob* believe that all plants have spirits, called *sip*. The *h-menob* handle the plants in ceremonies or use them to prepare herbal medicines. For these activities, they must first per-form ceremonies to enable them to work with the *sip* forces without being harmed. As they traverse the rainforest, they are cautious in dealing with an-imals who are protected by guardian spirits. They are also careful to recog-nize the spirits that appear as "winds," the *ik*. These spirits travel freely, according to the *h-men,* and can strike an individual in the body, causing ill-ness, or in the face or chest, causing death. Infant's heads are covered with sheets when they are carried from place to place to protect them from these forces and from the "evil eye." Very young children are said to be most vul-nerable to the "evil eye," which can cause uncontrollable crying (colic), di-arrhea, vomiting, and death. Babies sometimes wear small, wooden crosses of the *tancazche* tree on a wristlet or necklace to protect them. Treatments for the "evil eye" are practiced by some individuals in Coba. Children are said to succumb to the "evil eye" when the force of an adult's personality weakens the child. Persons who are hot and fatigued can transmit this illness and so can the gaze of a stranger. The concern for preventing this malady re-inforces a strong value in Maya culture. Individuals in the society must closely monitor their psychological and physical state. If a man is over-worked in the *milpa,* he must relax to regain a balance. Strangers who enter the village are considered threatening.

The Maya also identify individuals as *ikims*. These are the children born with double whirls of hair (double cowlicks) or who display double teeth, one behind the other. They are said to be able to "eat" their younger sib-lings. At night they grind their teeth while their younger brothers or sisters sicken, weaken, and possibly die. *Ikims* also may affect the health of their parents. The *K'ex* ceremony is held to remedy these situations. *H-men* carry out the ceremony, and as in many Maya ceremonies, one of the major components of the ritual is to provide substantial protein to the sick—in this case, cooked chicken. Another component of the rite is the transformation of the *ikim* to a "normal" state of being. The *ikim* is recreated as a doll of corn dough *(masa)*, clothed, and buried to "kill" the force that has possessed the child.

In considering the victim, the following facts may be significant. Analysis of the diet of Maya children and adults reveals that protein is a sporadic component of the diet. Most meat protein is included in the diet by chance (as from hunting), but its inclusion is also tied to economic wealth, that is, the ability to buy and breed chickens, turkeys, and pigs or the ability to purchase meat from a family that has an excess. Meat protein in the diet is desired by all, but it is occasionally limited because of economic constraints or bad luck. For nursing infants, protein is supplied by mother's milk, but an infant will drain the strength of the mother if her diet is substandard. In other words, for the Maya, dietary fluctuations can weaken the physical health of children and adults. The *K'ex* ceremony, as well as other rituals, alleviates this stress by providing a remedy (protein supplement) through formal action. The ceremony also places attention on the ailing individual, attention that increases the monitoring of individual welfare.

Another ceremony that replicates these actions is the *Chachac* rain ceremony. Rainfall patterns significantly affect the success or failure of *milpa* harvests. When the *milpa* is planted with corn seed in the late spring, if rains do not begin shortly the seeds fail to germinate. *H-men* carry out a *Chachac* ceremony yearly in the late spring to petition the *Chacob* or Rain Gods to bring the rains. The Maya harvest corn in the early fall. A good yield will provide corn for a family through the next year and, perhaps, an excess for long-term storage. A poor harvest may not provide even a full year's needs for a single family. The diet of the family would become stressed, and corn would have to be purchased. If corn stores are not sufficient for an entire year, by spring the diet will fall below that needed for maintenance. The Chachac ceremony provides a ritual setting and social activity to level out these deprivations. Part of the *Chachac* ceremony requires the sponsors of the ceremony to enter the forest and hunt deer that will be used in the ritual. Those families who can afford to will provide buckets of *masa* for making *nohua* (thick corn tortillas) and, perhaps, *pepita* (squash seed) to make a spread that is rich in protein. Since the entire community participates in the ceremony, feasting is an important source of protein for the entire population, but especially for those whose diet has been substandard. The protein is taken from those families most able to make contributions and is formally distributed to enhance the welfare of the entire community. The ceremonies of the Maya thus have two important functions: (1) to maintain the welfare of individuals and (2) to provide a setting where members of the community holding excess resources can contribute to the welfare of the entire social group in exchange for greater social prestige.

There are other ceremonies performed by the Maya that serve additional functions. The *Lolcatali* ceremony is carried out to protect towns from evil spirits that sweep through the towns as winds *(ik)* and attack individuals who walk streets or paths at night. The entire village participates in this ceremony carried out by the *h-men*. Shrines are set up to guard the village against evil spirits. The ritual has importance in that the entire community participates, thereby reinforcing social solidarity. The *Lolcatali* ceremony can also be held to protect individual houselots. If a house owner hears noises within the *solar* at night, an *h-men* is called to carry out this ritual.

The Maya also identify another spirit found in town or along paths in the forest, *xtabai*, a spirit in the form of a beautiful woman.

There was a boy, the story goes, who was intoxicated and, wandering through town, saw his girlfriend. She called to him, and he followed her out of town and into the forest. When they entered a cave, the boy realized that the form of his girlfriend was xtabai. *"Oh God," he cried out, and the form disappeared. In the morning,* milperos *found the boy, and he was crazy. When they brought him back to town, he fell sick with fever. The* h-men *was called, performed his rites, and cured the boy.*

Another time a man was walking at night along a path in the forest and came upon a beautiful woman. "Sit with me," she told him. When he sat down and touched her hand, it was ice cold. "This is xtabai," *he thought. He pulled out his knife and stabbed her with it and ran away down the path. The next day when he returned, he found his knife stuck into a nopal cactus. Here was the place where the spirit* xtabai *had waited for him.*

There are many stories about seeing the beautiful *xtabai*, morality stories which reinforce cultural values in Maya society—for example, "beware of drinking too much" and "take care traveling along forest paths in the night."

Other spirits that exist in the Maya world include the *alux* and the *tun*. The *alux* are dwarf-tricksters who live in *milpas*, and the *tun* are spiritual forces living in large limestone blocks. The *U-hanli-col* ceremony carried out in the *milpas* petitions these spirits to protect the fields from pests and animals that consume the crops. According to the *h-men*, if you do not hold this ceremony and provide *saca*, a ceremonial corn drink, for the *alux*, you will not have a good crop harvest. The ceremony is an interesting one that throws light on human–nature relations among the Maya. The *U-hanli-col* ceremony involves setting up a ceremonial table in the new cornfield and a series of walks through the field from the center to its four corners and then around the perimeter. In this way, following the *h-men*, the farmer carrying out this ceremony has an opportunity to walk over his field before he plants his seed. He can evaluate soil depth, types of soil within his cleared *milpa* area, and the best areas for planting corn, macal, or orchards. Although the farmer certainly would do this anyway, the ceremony ensures that his planning strategies are clear to him via a formal yearly ritual. Since most Maya ceremonies are communal activities (large numbers in some cases, but always more than a single individual), in the case of *U-hanli-col*, the farmer has access to a variety of opinions in creating the most productive planting possible for the specific field. In an area of considerable microecological variation, success in planting is enhanced by cooperation among peers in evaluating the landscape.

There are ceremonies to ensure the health of cattle *(Los Corrales)* and to protect the wild beehives *(U-hanli-cab)*. Both of these ceremonies encourage the monitoring and preserving of resources that enhance the economic welfare of the family.

In addition to tending the *milpas,* cattle, and bees, the Maya traditionally also moved into high rainforest to exploit the *zapote* trees for *chicle* (gum sap). In the past, *chiclero* camps were found throughout the eastern part of the Yucatan peninsula, and men signed on with sponsors who set up camps, provided cooks, and transported the *chicle* to centers in Cancun, Carrillo Puerto, and other eastern collection areas. The *chicleros* climbed the trees, cut the bark, and collected the sap in containers at the tree bottoms. Sometimes, a man's arm would be "hot," and he would have great success in collecting many liters of the gum sap. Sometimes, the man's arm would be "cold," and he would achieve little profit for his efforts.

If a *chiclero* was unable to collect large quantities of the sap and make a profit, while he worked he would call to the spirit of Juan del Monte, the guardian of the forest, owner of the *chicle:* "Where are you, Juan del Monte? I want to talk with you. Juan del Monte, come here. I am your friend." The *chicleros* said that when a man went alone into the forest to cut *chicle,* he might hear another person cutting the *zapote.* He would call to Juan del Monte. When he finished his work in one tree, he would climb down and see three cuts in another tree, way up high, and nothing else. If he cut that tree and put his sack on the bottom to catch the sap, it would fill three sacks, which was very productive. (It is unusual for one kilogram of sap to be drawn from a single tree, and the collection sacks hold 12 kilograms of *chicle.* If you fill three sacks—36 kilograms—from one tree, it is extraordinary.)

There was a man from Kanxoc who called to Juan del Monte. He heard someone cutting chicle *and went to the spot. There he saw a* zapote *with a few cuts in the bark way up high in the tree and nothing more. When he cut his tree, he filled three sacks with the sap. The next day, he returned to the spot early in the morning. There he met another man. The man had a beard and was covered with hair all over his body. The* chiclero *said, "You are Juan del Monte." The man said, "Yes, I am. I came because you called my name. I came to see why you called me the whole day long." The* chiclero *said, "You are the owner of* chicle. *I want you to give the sap to me. I want to work with you." Juan del Monte said to the* chiclero, *"Yes, let's work, but you must make a contract with me. For seven years, you must come and work with me during the* chicle *season." The* chiclero *agreed to do this. "Give me your machete, your rope, and your sacks. Exchange your tools with those of Juan del Monte."*

The chiclero *returned to cut* zapote *the next morning and found a tree that was marked by Juan del Monte. When he cut the bark, the sap ran and filled two sacks. When he had finished, Juan del Monte came to him and said, "Follow me. Here is another tree. Cut this one." When the* chiclero *did this, he filled four sacks with the sap. In three or four months, the man had made a great deal of money working with Juan del Monte. The next year, the* chiclero *returned to cut* chicle, *and the same thing happened. After the third year, during which he profited nicely again, the man was rich. After the sixth year of cutting* chicle, *the man thought, "If I go back the seventh year, I will never leave the forest." During the seventh year, the rich man stayed home.*

One night he was in his house, and at two o'clock in the morning, a man came to his door. "Who is it?" he cried out. The man responded, "I am your friend, don't you remember me?" The chiclero *said, "I don't have a friend. I'm sick, come back in the morning." The man said, "No, it's not possible. I'm going." The next night the man came back, but the* chiclero *refused to open the door. He knew who it was, and if he opened the door, he knew he would have to leave with Juan del Monte. The next night, the man came again. He said, "I'm your friend, open the door." The* chiclero *said, "I have no friend." Juan del Monte replied, "You had a friend when you were working. It was good to have a friend. You are going to come with me." The* chiclero *said, "You're crazy. My friends are my hands and my feet. I have no other friends." Then Juan del Monte left. The next night he didn't come back. A week passed, and he did not return. The* chiclero *thought that Juan del Monte had left, and he still had all of his money from cutting* chicle. *One day, the* chiclero *went to the plaza and stood near the church. A person came by leading three horses and asked him if he was interested in buying a horse. The price was reasonable, and the* chiclero *bought one. Then he went and bought a saddle for the horse. When he mounted the beast, he felt how strong it was. The horse ran well, ran strongly. He galloped to the plaza, and the horse ran faster and faster. As the man turned the horse toward his house, the horse fell and carried the man down. The man hit his head on a rock and instantly died. After the man's death, his family went to a* h-men *to ask why he had died and why his family had such misfortune. The* h-men *said that it was the man's destiny. He looked into a* sas, *a rock crystal, and saw that the man had made a contract with Juan del Monte. When the contract was broken, Juan del Monte pushed the feet of the horse and killed the man. The* h-men *saw what kind of friend the* chiclero *had made. Juan del Monte had cut off the life of the* chiclero.

It is said that many *chicleros* called to Juan del Monte, but "this spirit is evil, this is the devil." There are noises in the jungle near the *chiclero* camps—the spirit of Juan del Monte and the spirits of *chicleros* who have died doing this work.

The spiritual beings and forces that inhabit the Maya world provide a structure to explain the unexplainable, a setting to monitor individual psychic and physical health, a method to protect family resources, and a way to enhance social solidarity. Many of the cosmic forces structure the relationships between man and nature and reinforce or create a value system for life itself.

EPISODES IN TIME

Records of early occupation on the Yucatan peninsula date from before the Christian era. The Maya have occupied the peninsula for over 1000 years.

During the late Classic period (A.D. 600–900), the Maya of Coba had affiliations with the core Maya culture in the Peten of Guatemala to the south. During the early post-Classic period (A.D. 900–1200), Coba was in contact with the Itza of Chichen Itza to the west, and during the late post-Classic period (1200–1511 A.D.), the Lords of Coba vied with the rules of city-states in the lowlands to seat the Maya capital at Coba. Eventually Coba collapsed as a regional center, but in the 1850s the existence of the site was reported to John Stephens during his travels through Yucatan. In the 1950s, families from Kanxoc and Tixhualatun, Yucatan, migrated to the eastern Yucatan to cut *chicle,* hunt, and eventually plant *milpas,* settling around the lakes of Coba. The individuals and families who occupied Coba and related settlements during these periods are the Maya whose story is to unfold.

3/The Web of Kinship

Societies characterized as "kin-based" have been the focus of study by anthropologists for more than a century. The kinship system of the Maya has been described and analyzed, yet analytical problems remain. Perhaps there is too much information to codify it. Perhaps there is too little information from a native point of view. The Maya world resembles human societies everywhere, but the Maya pattern of kinship is unique.

The kinship system reinforces social status. Being born into one family or another provides each individual with a social position. Membership in a kinship group places each individual in time, with a past and a present, within a social group that insulates or protects the individual against changes, traumas, accidents, or nightmarish visions. The kinship group offers security and preserves important positions of power, knowledge, and skills. Fathers act as role models for their sons, and mothers teach their daughters appropriate skills. Survival skills are taught by the older generation to the younger generation. Kinship ties and a sense of community have enhanced the survival of the Maya through time.

Kinship, Family, and Society: The Pre-Columbian Order (A.D. 600–900)

The tropical sun reflected off the lime-plastered plaza fronting the temple of Ix Chebel Yax *as the gentle winds lifted ripples on the lakes. The white reflection blinded the members of the procession as the musicians tooted their horns and attendants fanned the ruler and his consort. Jaguar pelts and jade jewels hung from the ruler's shoulders. As the elite climbed the stairs to the court fronting the temple, jade earspools reflected the white light. The Lords of Coba had come to seat a new ruler and erect his stone portrait. In front of his statue was a round altar stone* (Figure 3.1). *The young ruler squatted over the stone, and taking a stingray spine, he grimaced and pressed it through his tongue. The royal blood collected in a stone bowl, and the blood tie to his ancestors was sealed.*

This line of rulers reached back in time to an ancestor that had become almost a shade. The blood of this ancient being, the founder of the royal kinship group, and that of his children was spent over altars signifying the web of kinship, the power of kinship, and the power of the Lords of Coba (Figure 3.2).

Figure 3.1. Stela with round altar in front of the Iglesia Pyramid, Coba.

The young ruler had earlier wed a beautiful young woman who had come *from the settlement of Naranjo to the south. Her lovely head had been elongated when she was an infant by being strapped to a cradle board, and her beautiful brown eyes were slightly crossed from the practice of hanging a jade bead on her*

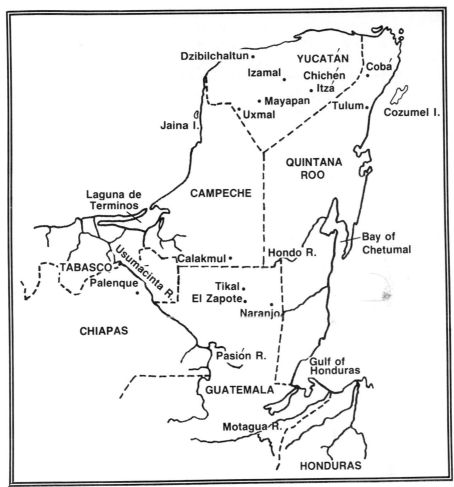

Figure 3.2. The lowland Maya—Pre-Hispanic period (A.D. *300–1441*).

nose. Her family was tied to the Maya kings of Tikal where Jaguar Paw, Curl Snout, and Stormy Sky had ruled. At Palenque, Pacal the Great had ruled for 68 years, and his mother, Zak-Kuk, had ruled before him. Chan Bahlum, Pacal's son, had ascended to the throne on his father's death.

At Coba, the elite bloodline had passed the rule from brother to brother, from father to son, or occasionally from father to daughter, forming a royal kinship group or royal lineage. The ruling ancestors were considered to be divine beings. In this way, the past controlled the future, for social position and responsibilities depended on name and the family's position.

The young ruler gazed at his wife. She carried their young son in her arms. The boy would be taught to worship his ancestors and to observe the sun, the moon, and the stars. He would learn the plant spirits that could be petitioned to cure the people of Coba. He would be taught to petition the gods and participate in rituals to call the Chacob, *the mighty Rain Gods. The goddess* Ix Chebel Yax *would reside in the temple, make the women fertile, and the crops ripen. The new lord thought "Someday my son will spill his blood and his seed and become Lord of Coba. Soon we must name him," he thought, "when the day is auspicious. Then, the priests will give him my name, and he will become a member of the* chi'bal, *my kinship group, my lineage. And he must take my wife's name, the* naal *name, and he will be a member of her kinship group. When he is older, we can send him south, and he can trade goods as I did, and when the time comes for him to rule, he will see far beyond the lakes of Coba." The young ruler pondered these thoughts as the ceremony continued. As darkness fell, candles were lit in the temple and around the new statue of the Lord of Coba. Here inscribed in stone was the record of his bloodline, his kinship, and his right to rule.*

At the corner of the pyramid, a small boy had fallen asleep. The festival day was long, and he had been awakened in the early morning. His father had worked carving the stone portrait of the ruler, and the boy had sharpened his father's tools. The work was arduous, but the boy was old enough to begin to learn the art. The statue needed to be rolled on logs to the temple, and his father supervised the work. He had shown the boy how the ropes and logs were worked, and the boy pushed and tugged with the other workers. Born into a family that had worked for the Lords of Coba for generation after generation, his fate was sealed. By birthright and by kinship, his social position was fixed or ascribed. "Perhaps I could become part of a trading expedition," the boy had dreamed. "Perhaps, then I could become something more. Or perhaps I could train for war and fight for my Lord. Then my position might be different."

Far from the plaza in a hut of pole and thatch, another young man pondered his future (Figure 3.3). As his wife and small son lay sleeping, by candlelight he planned his next day. His henequen bag was full of corn seed. "What luck that I was able to please the gods, and last year the harvest of corn and beans was so fine," he thought. "Perhaps this year I can gather some cacao *beans and begin to grow my orchard. My wife has planted the chile by the moon, and her mother helped her learn how to petition the spirits. Tomorrow, I plant my field. May the spirits help me. My father will come with the* h-men. *They will help me with the rites. My son will help me one day as I helped my father." His social position was fixed as the son of a* milpero. *He must clear the forest, plant the fields, harvest the crops, and feed his family.*

The ancient system of kinship among the Maya can be understood from studies by archaeologists and the deciphering of ancient Maya hieroglyphic inscriptions by epigraphers. Investigations have revealed the dynastic history of the ancient Maya rulers. According to Joyce Marcus (1976), pre-Columbian Maya monuments frequently show Maya lords holding anthropomorphic heads in the crook of their elbow or in their outstretched hand (Figure 3.1). These are probably ancestors, family emblems, or lineage markers. At the ancient Maya capital of Tikal, one prominent emblem is that of Scroll Baby appearing on the ruler's hips as an ancestral face marking a

Figure 3.3. Chuyche *(pole-and-thatch structure), Coba.*

ruling family. On the carved stone slab of Stela 31 at Tikal, Scroll Baby appears on the left hip of the Lord. Scroll Baby also appeared on the hip of a
ruler carved on Stela 1 at Tikal. The Scroll Baby emblem appears in the arm
of a woman on Stela 5 at the ancient site of El Zapote. This female from one
of the ruling families at the Maya capital of Tikal married the local lord of El
Zapote and was commemorated at the small site. The Scroll Baby motif
marks a royal kin group.

The ancient hieroglyphic inscriptions of the Maya that present emblems
shared by the royal elite reflect a unilineal descent system. Membership in a
kinship group was exclusively recognized through the father's kinship line.
The emblems in association with rulers perhaps represent esteemed ancestors, suggesting ancestor worship characteristic of lineal kin systems that are
apex oriented rather than ego oriented. The ancient portraits indicate that
kin affiliation was a mark of status in ancient Maya society. Both males and
females of royal lineages claimed legitimate rights to rule in major Maya capitals, and in addition, they provided superior status to local rulers through
links by marriage to important family groups.

Kinship, Chilam Balam, and the Katun *Prophecies (A.D. 1461–1559)*

Sacred books of the Yucatec Maya dating from the pre-Columbian period
were transcribed into European script. These books, the writing of Maya
prophets, were named after their most famous soothsayer, Chilam Balam,
the Jaguar Prophet. The *katun* prophecies predicted the coming of the Spani-

ards to the New World in 13 *Ahau* according to the Mayan calendar (Roys 1967, Edmunson 1982). The sacred books recorded information about the social order and disorder, power, and the politics of kinship.

The Itza of Chichen Itza had left that city and moved southeast. They visited Coba and moved farther south to another lake zone in the Peten. Kinchil Coba's ancestors welcomed them as nobles but were glad to see them leave. Although bloodletting had been practiced at Coba for generations, the Itza were ferocious and more blood thirsty than other groups. Mayapan had been sacked, and disorder had fallen over the land. Now, smaller states were organized, and once again people walked the Coba sacbe *with trade goods. Fish and other sea products were transported inland from Tulum, and great canoes were traveling along the east coast.*

"Our cotton is famous across the land, and the rites to musencabob, *the supernatural bees, are performed in the new temple. We are rich in honey for exchange," thought Kinchil Coba. "The* cacao *groves are producing well, but the sightings of great ships, flying ships, have been reported by the Lords of Cozumel. Could it be that the ancestor Kukulcan has come back as the Itza predicted, or is it new people who are arriving as the* katun *prophecies foretold. As ruler, I must continue the rites and send out more expeditions to trade and bring back news. This is the way my father and his father protected us, and it is my duty as Lord. Our family must continue to petition the ancestors. We have housed them to the east in Macanxoc. The candles are burning, and the priests guard their alcoves. The rains still water our fields, but the earth is tired now, and the gardens around the lakes are not producing as much as we need. My son is growing, yet as much as he is taught, there is a cloud that seems to cover him. The times are changing. I hope in his time, the gods will be kind, and he will rule well. I'm growing old, my vision is shattered. What gloom hangs over me. It is as though a great change is coming, but the soothsayers cannot predict what is to come. All I can see is fear in their eyes, a terror that is inexplicable."*

Away from the palace in the workshops, a young man is being taught to carve a monument of the old king's young son. The son will become king, and his position will be displayed on stone telling of his birth, his ascension to the throne, and ultimately, his death. As the young man works at carving the statue and the hieroglyphic text, he strikes the slab, and it cracks across the face of the young son who would be Lord of Coba. The crack runs through his own heart as through the text. In horror, the apprentice moves away from the slab. "This is my work and my family's work as it has been for generations. My father taught me as his father taught him these traditions. What have I done?"

On the edge of town, a young man rose in the early dawn. This morning he would search for the wild stingless bees. He would walk out in the forest with his father to find the hollow trunks where the musencabob *lived. In their wood houses, the bees produce their sweet honey. He and his father would find the trunks, and later in the night, they would return with torches, block the ends of the log with stones, gently lift it, and quietly carry it home. There they would guard the bees, a ritual would be made over the hive, and part of the honey would be brought to the priests at Ixmoja. The priests would use some of it, and the rest would be carried west or south by porters in exchange for the black obsidian from distant mountains. Perhaps, some of the obsidian would find its way to his house to be used, or perhaps, the traders would bring back flint axes to cut the forest for his* milpa. *He hoped that the sharp eyes of his father would find the bees. He would look for the* tancazche *tree and dig up the root. This would soothe the pain in his wife's tooth. Perhaps, his father's brother would go into the forest with him. His son was sick, and the old man knew which plants could be used to protect the boy and to cure his sickness. His wife was working over the fire, cooking thick tortillas for the men. She poured him a gourd cup full of pozole. This would fill his stomach, and she wrapped the tortillas in a cotton cloth. The men would pass his* milpa *and check for deer and wild pig tracks. Perhaps, tonight they would kill some game with the bow and arrow. Perhaps, the spirits of the forest would permit this. His life was the same as that of his father and that of his ancestors. Life would be the same for his boy.*

Kinship System in Transition: The Conquest and Colonial Rule (A.D. *1539–1810*)

Kinship systems provide indiv;duals with a place in the social system defined by birthright. All individuals enter the social world initially through family ties. Because family organization is responsive to historical circumstance and its organization reacts to ensure safety and security for any individual member, the kinship system of the Yucatec Maya most certainly would have responded to the invasion of the Yucatan peninsula and to the decimation of their population by the Spaniards beginning in the sixteenth century.

The Yucatec Maya population, as did native peoples everywhere in the New World, declined drastically during the first 100 years of contact with the Europeans. Perhaps the magnitude of population decline will never be known, but the heaviest losses probably took place during the earliest years of contact. European diseases were carried through the New World by European invaders or passed to native groups by Indian carriers moving through the outback. Population losses were massive and of a magnitude that qualifies as a "demographic catastrophe" (Farriss 1984, pp. 57–58). European diseases such as smallpox and measles were major killers. Famines during the colonial period leveled the population with declines estimated as killing as much as one third or more of the population. The peninsula was hit by locust plagues and hurricanes. There were droughts and typhus, yellow fever, and smallpox epidemics. People fell ill and died vomiting blood. These disasters were prevalent through the Colonial period, with reports on these holocausts dating from 1535 to 1810 (Farriss 1984).

Ah Kin, the Diviner, lay dying in the priests' compound. His swollen body, covered with a rash, was wasting away. Medicines were prepared, he was bathed, concoctions were massaged over his body, he was given potions to drink, and he had laid in the sweat baths, but still his body was wasting away. He had been able to give instructions for curing rituals, but now that he burned with a fever, he could no longer instruct the priests in ritual nor in other cures. As he lay dying, he thought of the mysterious illnesses that were plaguing his people. Since his people had received reports of the landing of men on the eastern coast and Nahuatl traders had reported that the dzulob (foreigners) had marched on the capital of Moctezuma, the illnesses had come as though carried by the winds. The priests had lain dying, and their numbers were greatly diminished. The traders had carried the king's eldest son back home on a litter, and he had died from the plague. Whole families had become ill and died, and families were moving out of the city into the forest to escape. With the king's eldest son dead, his younger son began the rites to assume the throne. The old king, grief stricken with the loss of his son, his two daughters, and his wife, was incapable of ruling. The younger son, a fine and brave warrior, took on the burden of controlling a population mad with grief. In his delirious condition, the old priest, Ah Kin, cursed the gods. His mind burning, he saw the world of the dead and dreamed of a multitude of his people entering the Underworld. His last thoughts were of the living, the chaos, the destruction of the web of kinship that had cemented Maya society for a thousand years.

Beyond the center of the city in a pole-and-thatch structure. Bach Can (Chachalaca Snake) leaned over the body of his dead wife and prayed softly. His beautiful wife, their dead infant daughter cradled in her arms, lay on the floor of his house. He had prepared the grave, would lay her in it, and would place some corn and a single jade bead with her. His crops were lost this year to the rains and the winds. The insects had eaten his fields. Most of his family had died from the plague and he would leave this place, where he felt such sadness, with his father and two brothers. They would move into the forest and collect the fruit of the wild pich *tree to make bread, dig up the roots of* cup *(wild jicama), and eat the fruit of the wild* cumche. *With his male kinsmen, he would cut the forest and plant the sacred corn. The* dzulob *were coming and he would escape into the forest. There his father, his brothers, and he would petition the ancestors to protect them. They would hold rites to protect their fields, would call the* Chacob, *the Rain Gods, and would worship* musencabob *when they found the beehives and sacks of honey. His house would be left behind, but his Maya culture would survive in the forest through the web of kinship.*

In the early 1550s, the Spaniards instituted a colonial policy of congregation of Indians into controllable settlements. The Spaniards made every effort to gather the fugitive Maya by luring them back to villages with false promises that foods would be supplied. This corralling probably contributed to the Indians' starvation, low fertility, and population reductions (Farriss 1984). With the massive population decline and the disruption of customs, the Maya began to innovate to maintain life. Survival strategies introduced new elements of kinship organization into the cultural repertoire.

The holpop, *head of the Canche lineage, master of the men's house, or* popolna, *staggered into Kanxoc with his small group of followers. The group was weak from hunger, too ill to travel on, and the foreigners had captured them with promises of food. "Perhaps the family could survive here in the small village. We could build a family compound here, work together, and live," thought La-hun Canche. His wife had died from the plague and he brought his family to town to find a new wife. He knew that the Caamal family lived in town and that they had intermarried with the Canche lineage before the plague. In fact, the small group included one daughter of the Caamal lineage who had married La-hun Canche's eldest son. The small group included members of the Canche, Caamal, Chan, Xoc, and Cocom lineages. The holpop had absorbed these strag-glers into his family. "The family," he thought "is fragmented now because of the deaths of so many members from the plague. We have suffered from the ven-geance of our gods, and our crops were destroyed by diseases."*

Yet, the force of famine, illness, death, and other disasters were com-monplace to those living under the tropical canopy. The extended family protected them; it was their only defense.

The Spanish colonial authorities divided extended families, insisting that each married couple establish a separate household, and the Spanish author-ities encouraged marriage at an early age. However, colonial census materi-als indicate that multiple-family residential compounds were common. The Maya resisted the imposed reorganization, and families settled in contiguous houselots as they most probably did in pre-Hispanic times. Reversion to ex-tended family compounds was accomplished by the Maya whenever or wherever Spanish supervision was lax. In 1583, 93% of the households in Tizimin were multiple-family residences, and as late as 1815, census material on ranchos around the town of Bolonpoxche, parish of Uman, notes that all ranchos had three or more adults or were organized as extended family units (Farriss 1984). Thus, adjustment to life under the tropical canopy retained an extended family organization that enhanced the Maya's social, economic, and perhaps, political welfare.

The older pattern of marriage among the Maya, whereby newly married couples lived in the bride's family compound where the groom worked tem-porarily for his father-in-law (*haancab* or bride service), was abolished by Spanish law, which required independent households to be established on marriage. It was no longer permitted for the young couple to move into the extended family unit of the male's relatives after the bride service. In addi-tion, the Spaniards imposed tribute and head tax payments on every married male. Thus, the newly married couple, both males and females, were bur-dened with payments when their economic wealth was minimal. The Spani-ards also encouraged early marriage to control sexual misconduct. Early marriage may have contributed to increasing the birth rate among the Maya, but the tax and tribute system imposed on newly married couples may have been such a burden that it contributed to infant mortality. Spanish intrusion and restructuring of Maya family organization may have inhibited, rather than enhanced, Maya population recovery in the Yucatan (Farriss 1984, p. 173).

   The older traditional system of extended family organization along the patrilineal or male descent line, with filial obligations and ancestor worship, was steadily undermined by the system imposed by the colonial authorities: nuclear family households with bilateral inheritance patterns. Forced congregation of Maya families into larger towns was matched by the Maya response of out-migration from these population centers. The Maya always had one option in their dealings with political or ecclesiastic powers. They could slip into the tropical forest, and the canopy, the vines, and the thicket would cover their tracks. The Maya used the forest as an exit to escape from any internal friction. The Spaniards unwittingly encouraged this option by diluting the ties any nuclear family had to a larger extended family (Farriss 1984, p. 198).

   The Maya dispersal or reversal of the congregation program was underway as early as the 1580s. Indians were migrating into the bush and establishing ranchos. The ranchos were rarely, if ever, the houses of single individuals or even single nuclear families. These were groups of several nuclear families, usually brothers, a father and his grown sons, or other patrilineally related males replicating the old kinship pattern. Life in the bush diminished the effective authority of parish priests and town officials, permitting traditional kinship elements to survive through time.

Lahun Canche and his family had lived in Kanxoc for the past ten years. The old man had seen changes through these years. As Lahun Canche entered the end of his life, he thought more and more about the past and wondered about the future. Already, the colonial authorities had summoned him to Saci (Valladolid) for a hearing and told him that his sons must move out of his household with their wives and young children. They told him that he must find a husband for his 12-year-old daughter and that his 14-year-old son must take a wife. No longer would his sons serve in the household of their fathers-in-law on marriage, but they must set up separate households. Lahun Canche pondered these changes and the fragmentation of his family. "How would my sons and their families survive alone?" he thought. "They must work collectively to farm, collect the beehives, watch the animals, tend the garden, and plant fruit trees." His daughter was a child, and his young son could never manage a household on his own. He questioned how families could be tied together if the new son-in-law no longer worked for the father of his new wife. "Families cannot survive alone under the tropical canopy," Lahun Canche reasoned. "Your parents, your in-laws, and your brothers were the guardians of your life. Your economic welfare depended on these kinsmen. You could never cut the forest, burn it, sow it, and harvest it alone." Lahun Canche pondered these changes and wondered what the future would bring. The old man stood up and called to his younger son, "Go and bring the family here to me. I have to talk with them now." The young son walked off to gather the family and returned with his elder brothers, his younger sister, the wife of his father, and the wives of his married brothers. The small children stood near their parents. Sixteen members of the family came to hear what the old man had to say. "We are leaving," the old man whispered. "If we stay, we will die and will not be able to work and live as a family. If we stay and pay trib-

*ute and head tax, there will be nothing left, we will be alone, and we cannot survive. We are leaving, going into the forest. The forest will protect us. We can survive in the forest. My sons, you are old enough to work with me in the forest, cut it, plant the land, and harvest the crops. We will plant trees and harvest their fruits. The wives will cook for us, plant their gardens, and take care of the children. My wife knows many of the herbal cures for sickness, and I know the rites to petition the gods to protect us. We are leaving, and we will leave tonight."
The old man turned and entered his house. There, he dug a hole in the corner and recovered a clay mask. This was an alux, and he gently wrapped it in a cotton cloth (Figure 3.4). "The alux will protect us," he thought. "I will bury it again when we build a new house in the bush. We will survive there, and our customs will survive through time."*

Compadrazgo

One element of kinship introduced by the Spaniards did serve Maya interests and was adopted by them: the *compadrazgo* system, or the Hispanic system of god parenthood. Clearly, the Maya lifeway demanded cooperation

Figure 3.4. Ceramic alux with his foot and part of his sandal found in the Ruins of Coba.

and reciprocal aid beyond the limits of the nuclear family. During the pre-Columbian period, life's trials were controlled by membership and participation in extended families that insulated individuals against the contingencies of life. The Colonial period intensified life's problems by the introduction of epidemic diseases, the burdens of taxation, and demands by priests for *limosnas* (alms) or *obvenciones* (head taxes). The cushion of extended family or the relief it offered from birth to death was ripped away from the Maya by Spanish administrative command. Although evidence suggests that Spanish efforts to restructure family organization were resisted by the Maya, massive population decline left some individuals without extended family groups, not according to the law but because of famine or disease. A patrilineal kin group could be entirely wiped out, and the Maya responded by deviating from their rules of patrilineal inheritance because there were no heirs. The Spaniards introduced the standard Catholic concept of god parenthood. The Maya reworked the concept to recreate kinship bonds, extend kinship networks, and recreate the old system of ties (Farriss 1984; pp. 256–262). Now, the Maya could ensure their individual and corporate survival. Individuals could and did create kinship bonds sanctified through ritual on their own.

The godparenthood system entailed a ritual bond established in a ceremony that tied an adult sponsor to a child. This guardianship, as it has been explored, was an illusion because the important tie was between natural parent and godparent or between *compadres* or *comadres,* the set of adults. Under the Spanish system, the same godparents often served as sponsors for all of the godchild's rites of passage (that is, baptism, communion, and confirmation). In the Spanish colonies, the Maya altered the *compadrazgo* system, and it became much more elaborate. The system was used to create not merely a single guardian for a child, but multiple ties to many sponsors—not only for a guardianship for children, but to satisfy the needs of adults by creating extended "kin" and social, economic, and political ties. The common ritual occasions were observed, but many other events, some of which had little spiritual focus, were also celebrated; for example, the first time a child is seated on the mother's hip, or *hetzmek,* the first tooth, the 15th birthday, and so on (see Nutini 1984). With epidemic disease and famine prevalent during the Colonial period, the *compadrazgo* system created the social bonds to replace or supplement ties that no longer existed. There was an emphasis on *compadre* links between men, but women were also linked, as *comadres,* through the godparenthood ceremonies. Thus, the *compadrazgo* system reinforced the old patrilineal bias.

KINSHIP IN MODERN TIMES (A.D. 1950s–1980s)

In the 1950s, Don Silvestre May and his brothers came from Kanxoc to Coba to cut *chicle* to sell in Valladolid. The brothers entered the forest around the Coba lakes and saw that there were plenty of deer and other animals to hunt. There were stands of *zapote* to cut for *chicle*. Here was rich black soil for agricultural fields. The men worked together and cut the forest, burned it, and planted their *milpas*. When the harvest was ready, five families moved from Kanxoc to Coba with Don Silvestre. Don Panfilo Canche was among these first men to move to Coba to stay. He was married to Don Silvestre's daughter, Juliana. Don Jose Maria Caamal Uh came from Kanxoc. He and Don Silvestre were *compadres*. During this early period, other men came from Tixhualatun. Don Dolores Cen, Don Fernando Cen, and Bernabel Cen moved to Coba from Tixhualatun. Pedro Celestino Noh and his wife, who was Don Silvestre's daughter, moved to Coba from Kanxoc (Figure 3.5). Arturo Chimal and Don Silvino Uicab also moved to Coba from Kanxoc. Teodoro May walked from Kanxoc with his wife, his children, and his pigs (Figure 3.6). It took him two days to get to Coba, where his wife's grandfather and his uncles had *milpas*. Through the 1960s, 1970s, and 1980s, additional families, mainly from Kanxoc, Tixhualatun, and Chemax migrated to settle in Coba. A few families came from Valladolid, Tizimin, Chichimila, Ticuch, and Yalcoba.

The Form of the Family

Don Silvestre was tired. Through the morning, his eldest son, his son-in-law, and his step-son had worked with him to plant their milpa. *Last year's harvest had been very good, and the best seed had been kept for planting this year. Don Silvestre thought how lucky he was to have two strong sons and a willing son-in-law to help him. The extra hands made it possible to cut more forest, burn it, sow it, and harvest it. He thought about his family. His eldest daughter was a competent herbalist, taught by her mother to use the plants. His son-in-law also was quite able in using the plants to cure illness. Don Silvestre thought, "The two of them will guard the health of this family." His son was an able gardener and had planted fruit trees. The* cacao *trees he had planted would be used for chocolate drinks, and the* jicara *trees he had planted would provide bowls and cups from its hard-shelled fruit. His son's wife had planted cotton, and she knew how to make thread and weave it into hammocks. In addition, his step-son was collecting wild bees so that they would have honey to sweeten their foods. Don Silvestre leaned back, rested in his hammock, and thought, "My sons will help me as I helped my father. Together we will survive."*

Don Silvestre and his eldest son walked to the temple of Ix Chebel Yax. *The ancient temple was in ruins, but fronting the stairs stood the stone slab with an ancient ruler's portrait—and in front of this, a round altar stone. Don Silvestre knelt down and placed two candles on the altar. He began to recite a simple prayer asking the* Dueño del Monte *(Owner of the Forest) to protect him and his son when they entered the forest to hunt that night. When he finished the prayer, Don Silvestre glanced at his son. He knew that his son had heard the prayer before, and although they never spoke of it, Don Silvestre knew that his son would also recite the prayer someday to protect him and his own son when they entered the forest to hunt. This ritual was only one of several that Don Silvestre had taught his son.*

Figure 3.5. Pedro Celestino Noh.

The Itza family had left Valladolid and moved southeast. They settled on a rancho near the village of Coba. Don Lorenzo brought his wife, four sons, and two daughters into the forest. He worked to clear and plant the land. Life was very hard in those early years. His family was large, with many mouths to feed,

Figure 3.6. Teodoro May Chi.

and he and his wife were the only labor force. They worked the land, raised chickens, kept a few pigs and a few head of cattle. They planted fruit trees, had a small garden, and kept wild bees. They were rich in honey and sold it. They grew cotton, and his wife wove their hammocks. When his eldest son could help him in the milpa, *the extra hands made life easier. Now, his eldest son worked the rancho, and Don Lorenzo and another son worked at their store in town. Three sons worked at the big hotel in town. "We are prosperous now," thought Don Lorenzo Itza, but he remembered how hard life had been on the land. "It is because of my sons," Don Lorenzo was sure, "that our family had prospered." By working collectively, the Itza family had thrived.*

Nicolas Caamal Canche, his wife and his seven children lived in the small village of Coba (Figure 3.7). His father had settled in the village but had subsequently moved away to Chemax, leaving his son, Nicholas, to guard his house and his cattle. The plague had hit the cattle, and many animals died or were sold. When Nicolas' younger brother moved into the village to live in the father's house, Nicholas, Maria, and their children built a new house. The younger brother sold his father's remaining cattle and the enclosed rancho to another man in town and then moved away. Nicholas also sold his own cattle at that time. Nicholas thought, "I'm alone. None of my family lives in Coba. There is no one to protect me, and no one lives here to whom I can turn for assistance. I must ask Jose Isabel to be godparent to my young daughter. We must become compadres. *He is an honest man. He is a curer. If he will serve as godparent, our friendship will be cemented."*

Figure 3.7. Nicolas Caamal Canche.

Bilateral Cross-Cousin Marriage

In the 1930s, Fred Eggan (1934) suggested that bilateral cross-cousin marriages may have been formed among the Yucatec Maya in former times (the male seeking a wife from the set of his father's sister's daughters or mother's brother's daughters). If this hypothesis is true, it would be the only documented example of this type of marriage pattern in Middle America. Research on this peculiar feature of kinship and marriage organization may answer the question, Why did the Maya organize their social world in this fashion? More precisely, one can look at this pattern by assessing how the system enhances the quality of life for the Maya.

In a community such as Coba, with a small number of families, most of whom came from two small towns in Yucatan or a few other small towns, the total number of possible mates is restricted. In such communities, where individuals are born into societies in which kinship ties (biological, marriage bonds, or fictive kin ties) represent the social fabric, it would not be impossible to select a wife from the members of one's kindred or from one's mother's or father's extended family.

Marsela Tus Canche was 11 years old when Alfonso Chic Tus asked her father if he could marry her. He was her cousin, and she had known him all her life. His mother and her father were sister and brother. Alfonso Chic Tus married his matrilateral cross-cousin. Alicia Chimal May married Elias May Chimal. They were cousins. Elias' mother and his wife's father were siblings. Elias married his matrilateral cross-cousin.

It appears that the mother's brother's daughter may be selected as a marriage partner. Why would the Maya select this marriage pattern? First, the pool of marriageable females is small. Second, if a lineal descent system is operating, the cross-cousin is not considered a member of an individual's lineage. Last, cementing kinship and marriage ties with groups in which the husband's and wife's parents are members and have extended ties enhances the welfare of the newlywed couple.

Postmarital Residence Patterns

Postmarital residence patterns may contribute to the economic vitality of newlywed couples. In Coba, data were compiled on 47 families with respect to residence of couples on marriage. Only two couples lived in the household compound of the bride's family when married (the *haancab* pattern) whereas 16 couples lived with the husband's family (patrilocal residence pattern). Of 47 families, 29 couples responded that they set up neolocal households or independent households separate from both sets of parents on their marriage. Were these neolocal residences isolated from the family? Did the newlyweds lives in the same town? Could they call on the husband's or wife's family for assistance? And did they? This review of postmarital residence patterns reveals that of those who created new households, only three couples settled in homes isolated from the husband's or wife's families. Nine newlyweds settled in the same village as the husband's parents whereas five couples resided in the same village as the wife's parent. Ten newlyweds resided in the village where both sets of parents lived. (Two couples did not provide sufficient information to determine the postmarital residence pattern.) The general conclusion is that Maya newlywed couples are isolated from extended kin only in rare or exceptional circumstances. In fact, 89–94% of the newlyweds were living near either one or both sets of their parents.

Kinship and Adaptation to Life Under the Tropical Canopy

The modern Yucatec Maya kinship system evolved out of elementary forms of kinship dating back to the pre-Columbian and Colonial periods. In modern times, the options open to the Maya to create a kinship network are considerable and build flexibility into the social, economic, and political system. The ancient kin groups emphasized the patrilineage or the family of the male. For the modern Yucatec Maya peasants, the advantage of solidified male relations is that they enlarge the labor force available to each family.

The ancient kinship system also recognized the contributions that could be made by the female's kin group, and among the modern Maya a couple may choose to reside with either the groom's family or the bride's family. Traditionally, couples were obligated to reside with both families. Grooms served their fathers-in-law with *haancab* (bride service) on marriage, and the couple later resided with the groom's family.

Ultimately, the married pair set up an independent household adjacent to the male's parents. The advantage of this postmarital residence pattern is that it permits the newlywed couple slowly to build up their economic resources, provides a support system in the earliest stages of their marriage, and incorporate their labor into a system that is beneficial to all.

Another ancient pattern of family organization was the formulation of extended rather than nuclear families. A male or female head of the household would live with his or her unmarried children, his or her married children, the spouses of these children, and their grandchildren. Brothers also formed fraternal extended households (Figure 3.8). The advantage of this extended form of the family derives from the fact that success under the tropical canopy depends on the amount of labor available to each family. The larger the family, the greater the chance that during its development, the family would have sufficient hands to work to secure its own basic needs. Of 53 families now living in Coba, 11 are extended family units.

Nuclear family organization is another option open to the Maya. It is an option that is apparently a spatial design only, for social ties to real or fictive kin are maintained and fostered. Of 53 families interviewed, 42 families lived in walled *solares* (yards) as nuclear families. However, most households that were spatially isolated within a walled houselot were not at all socially isolated. Grandparents, parents, brothers, sisters, and children of siblings were living nearby within the village. Only nine families in the village were organized truly as nuclear families, and most of these (seven) were recent migrants to the settlement and had lived in Coba for only one or two years. In

Figure 3.8. The household of Alonso Cen, his family, and his brother's wife.

time, marriage alliances and *compadrazgo* relationships will absorb these families into the extended kin organization.

The web of kinship among the Yucatec Maya through time has adapted and adjusted to life under the tropical canopy. The royal lineages recorded in stone and dating to the pre-Columbian period served to organize power around the system of kinship. In ancient Coba, family networks served to socialize a child or train new societal members for their lifetime work as ruler, artisan, or *milpero*. Economic life was organized through kinship. Families were the loci of knowledge about the spirit world, and sacred and ceremonial life was organized around the family.

Large, extended families were able to work cooperatively with sufficient labor to cut, fire, and plant their fields, tend their bees, and make their clothes or other necessities using natural resources and human labor. Bride service and patrilocal residence (subsequent residence with or near the family of the groom) permitted elder kin to assist newlywed couples and to cement social relationships. Large extended families with a large number of males adapted successfully to life in the rainforest.

With the arrival of the Spaniards and the associated demographic catastrophe in the sixteenth century, the Maya rapidly adopted the Hispanic *compadrazgo* or godparenthood system to recreate an extended kinship system of economic, social, and spiritual security. However, the pressure of the Spanish overlords on the indigenous Maya was diffused because the Maya always had and frequently took the option of fleeing into the forest with a set of male kinsmen or *compadres*. Isolated ranchos, especially in the eastern sector of the Yucatan peninsula, preserved the traditional web of kinship (see Villa Rojas 1945).

From the earliest records dating to the pre-Columbian period, evidence points to the migratory nature of the Maya, moving from site to site, sometimes moving in response to natural demands, sometimes migrating because of social pressures or opportunities, and finally, sometimes moving because of cosmic directive (see Edmunson 1982). These migrations affected the web or network of kinship. Sometimes, the kinship ties were strengthened, as in the case of some families in modern Coba who came to live in the area with their sons, daughters, daughters-in-law, and sons-in-law. Sometimes, kinship ties were broken when nuclear families moved into a new village and when the family of the husband and the bride remained elsewhere. However, the Maya thrived through time, and their elaborate and tolerant system of kinship perhaps contributed to their welfare. The Maya are intensely social and reach out to incorporate individuals into their social network, slowly but firmly hinting at, requesting, and requiring social reciprocity. Perhaps, kinship is the most profound or elementary form of reciprocity—mothers give their milk, and the children return their love (respect). For the Yucatec Maya, reciprocity of action and redistribution of goods have been and continue to be embedded in the web of kinship. According to Farris (1984), the themes of reciprocity and redistribution have led to strong ties of kinship and to community and the collective survival of the Maya.

4/Economic Production and Exchange

ECONOMIC ORGANIZATION

In the Maya lowlands, the basic social unit producing and consuming goods is the family. However, the nuclear family has rarely been able to provide fully for its own welfare and has exchanged goods and labor with relatives or friends to enhance or ensure survival. This direct or reciprocal exchange has permitted Maya farmers to survive in an unpredictable environment, with some years too sunny, others too dry, with hurricane storms that flatten crops, or insect plagues that consume plants. Under these conditions, the small nuclear family has found security for its members in a broad social network of kinsmen and friends.

At times, the larger social groups among the Maya, either kinship groups or territorial units, have been mobilized and organized to alleviate economic stress. Food resources were collected, centralized, and distributed to group members. The groups may be large kin groups, barrio neighbors, or members of an entire community. The most apparent and prevalent examples of collection and redistribution of food took place during the traditional ritual celebrations that the Maya observed as part of the annual agricultural cycle. However, these celebrations were not the only means by which goods were redistributed to ensure the collective welfare of the Maya. It was also possible and necessary to acquire goods from commercial markets, stores, and itinerate traders. To comprehend the social organization among the Maya, one must understand the framework of their economy, built within the ecological constraints and possibilities offered by the tropical rain forest.

ECOLOGY AND ECONOMY: THE ANCIENT ORDER (A.D. 600–900)

A young man lived far from the central plaza in a hut built of poles lashed together by vines. The anicab *vines would last more than a* katun *if they stayed dry. The roof was a thick thatch of* guano, *its fan-shaped leaf dried, crushed, and woven into a stick frame. The thatch roof kept out the torrential rains of the wet growing season and provided a thick insulation against the sun of the dry season. He had worked to build the hut himself with a little help from his father and his older brother. They had worked together on his house as they did in other tasks to ensure the welfare and the survival of his family. At the outside corners of his hut, he and his son had built a small garden area. Rich, black soil was hauled in baskets and dumped inside an area bounded by logs. Here, his wife had planted chile to season their soup. She planted* apazote *and* chaya, *among other medicinal herbs, and a little tobacco. His mother lived in a hut across the yard, worked her gardens, and planted* achiote *(to color and flavor food), tomatoes, and cotton. His eldest brother's wife grew* celantro *(coriander) and had a small plot of* nal *(fast-growing corn) near the house. The three families shared these garden products, freely exchanging in a general and reciprocal fashion. The women tended the gardens, watered them every three days if they needed to do so, and supplemented the diet with condiments that everyone enjoyed.*

Behind his house was a pen built of woven saplings (cololche). *Inside the pen was a young deer that he had caught one night hunting in the forest. The animal had been feeding with its mother in his cornfield, and he had speared the doe and captured the fawn. The slain doe was prepared, and its meat shared with the family and the nearest neighbors. The rich venison made a tasty meal, a much-valued variety in the diet. Perhaps, the fawn would be used in the upcoming ceremony as a sacrifice to the Sky Gods. Perhaps, his wife would care for it and fatten it. and it could be sacrificed another time (see Pohl and Feldman 1982).*

He heard someone coming and turned to see his father stepping on the stones that marked the dry pathway between his father's old and large house and his new and modest chuyche *(pole-and-thatch hut). His father greeted him and told him to come and check the stack of tree trunks at his house. The slender trunks were stacked on a rack, and within them were the stingless honey bees, or* colecab (Figure 4.1). *Today, he and his father would extract honey, take it to the center of Coba, and present it to the priests in the temple. When the honey had been presented, the priests would speak to the gods to ensure that honey would be produced through the next year. This year was so dry and the rains so short and slight that the flowers had been fewer than in other years and honey production was low. Perhaps, the gods would be more generous in the next year. While walking, he and his father passed fruit-bearing trees that had been planted in the yard area. He plucked a fat avocado, sliced it open with a flint knife, and offered half to his father. Together, they headed for the beehives to begin their work.*

Nearer to the center of the city by a small stone house, a young boy was working with his father. They both were squatting on a stone platform in front of their sleeping quarters. They were stone cutters and were pecking basalt imported from the highlands far to the south to make metates *or grinding slabs. The finest* metates *were the three-legged ones but were difficult and time consuming to make. Others were simple slabs, and a few were very small. The miniature ones were used to grind chile or were deposited in caves as offerings to the gods.*

The Lords of Coba brought the basalt back from trading expeditions to the south. The material was stored in the center of town, and stone cutters from different barrios in the town received the raw material and produced the finished product. Cruder metates *were pecked from limestone* (Figure 4.2). *The boy and his father made these, as well—tapping a sharp tip of flint against the soft lime-*

Figure 4.1. Tree trunks used as hives for the stingless honeybees, the colecab.

Figure 4.2. Limestone metate.

stone block. Sometimes, they would have trouble distributing these for sale, and they would lay around in the yard.

The boy and his father relied heavily on the Lords of Coba to acquire raw materials. Although they cut limestone blocks with water and with sand and used flint knives to form the metates, *the basalt was available only from the traders who brought it to the Lords of Coba.*

In the center of town, the Lord of Coba, the halach uinic, *received word that traders were entering Coba over the south* sacbe. *His messenger had informed him that the traders were loaded with products. The ruler was pleased that his trading partners to the south appreciated the value of his trade item—his younger sister, sent south to marry a* batab *(governor) of a distant town. He hoped the marriage would permit a more favorable flow of goods. Tied by marriage, the* batab *would conform more easily to trading demands. The Lord of Coba would send the* batab *honey and beautiful woven cotton cloth made by his people. Along the trade route, he would receive basalt, obsidian, and the blue-green quetzal bird feathers that were of a sacred color and valued so highly. He thought to himself that with these connections he might again offer women, perhaps the most valued trade item, for the items most needed. In the famine years, he could demand food from these southern connections. He prepared himself to welcome the traders. Wrapped in his cotton cloak, with an elaborate headdress of feathers on his head, he was handed a staff that marked his royal standing, and he walked out into the sunlight to meet the traders. Some of the goods would be placed in storehouses, and other items would be redistributed to his people. This would give him prestige in their eyes and power to demand more tribute from them. For the Lord of Coba, all economic production and exchange were translated into the power to rule.*

THE ANCIENT ORDER: THE EVIDENCE

The ancient system of economics among the Maya of Coba can be discerned from the archaeological record, carved stone monuments, and frescoes. Analysis of these remains provides evidence of the practice of reciprocity and redistribution for the exchange of goods and services. The ancient settlement patterns show the concatenation of households, perhaps indicating a cluster of nuclear families intimately interacting. If nuclear families of different generations (perhaps a man, his father, and his eldest brother) were living together, then they probably shared goods and exchanged labor in a generalized reciprocal fashion as do families everywhere. From the ancient houselot walls in the residential precincts of Coba, bits and pieces of obsidian have been excavated. Obsidian or volcanic glass is not native to the Yucatan, so it must have been traded for and transported to Coba. In the ancient city, the elite probably controlled the redistribution of obsidian to the general population. Other commodities also had a restricted circulation. Feathered headdresses were probably reserved for the elite members of society, and pearls, stingray spines, and spondylus shells were brought to

Coba by long-distance traders and kept by the elite, buried in caches, and perhaps dedicated to the gods. The organization of economic specializations among the ancient Maya has been a controversial issue. Some scholars have argued for a greater degree of specialization (Adams 1970; Becker 1973; Kintz 1983) than others (Sanders 1973; Webster 1985; Abrams 1987). Although this argument cannot be settled with currently available data, the mechanics of exchange and the behavior of individuals probably encompassed reciprocal and redistributive modes. These modes of exchange, though changing perhaps in importance, have survived into the modern period to ensure the collective welfare of the Yucatec Maya.

THE ECONOMIC SYSTEM IN TRANSITION: THE CONQUEST AND
COLONIAL RULE (A.D. 1539–1810)

The Spanish intrusion into the Yucatan Peninsula (Figure 4.3) was quite unlike the Spanish conquest of Central Mexico. Hernando Cortés marched on the Aztec capital of Tenochtitlan in the Valley of Mexico, and within two years, he had reduced the city to rubble. One of Cortés lieutenants, Francisco de Montejo, and Montejo's son, required two full decades to conquer the Yucatec Maya (Farriss 1984, p. 12). Part of their problem was that the Spanish soldiers saw nothing worth conquering and therefore deserted the Montejos. Another part of the problem was that the Maya refused to remain conquered (see Reed 1964; Bricker 1981; Farriss 1984; Wells 1985).

The ecological setting of the Yucatan made the Spanish conquistadors ill-suited to pitch battle. In their coats of armor, they clattered over limestone boulders, slipped into holes, tripped across a pitted landscape on horses, and were lashed or hung by vines and branches. The Maya, however, moved along well-known trails on foot, slipping easily through the forest. When the Spaniards forced the Maya to comply, the Maya readily agreed to the colonial plan. As soon as the Spaniards were out of sight, the Maya turned again to their ageless traditional lifeways. The sun, the moon, and the movement of seasons influenced Maya life considerably. Traditional social bonds ensured survival. The ideological framework, translated into ceremony and tradition, influenced how the Maya interacted with each other and with the natural world that surrounded them.

Lahun Canche was living in the small village of Kanxoc with his children and grandchildren. He was a milpero. On this day, he picked up his henequen fiber bag full of corn seed and beans and headed out to his col (milpa) to plant seed. He listed out all the foods he enjoyed eating and made plans for cultivating them together in his field. The field would look like a miniature forest when he was through and would have the best chance of producing the most for Lahun and his family. He carried his xul (digging stick), to press holes in the rich box luum (black soil), and from the bag of seeds, he would drop a few seeds at a time in the holes. He would also plant some squash with the corn and beans. Nearby,

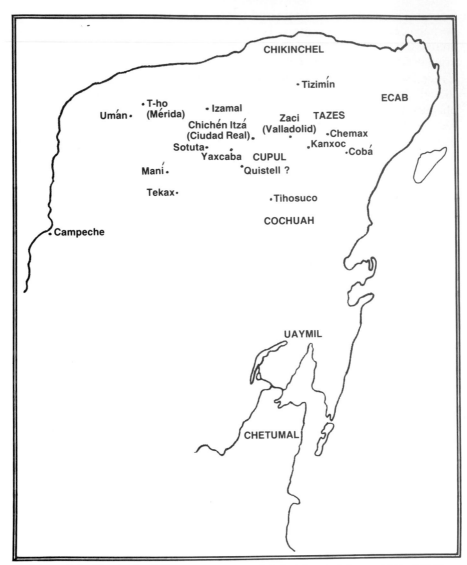

Figure 4.3. The lowland Maya—conquest and Colonial periods (A.D. 1441–1821).

he would plant chile pepper. Root crops would grow in his milpa, and he would plant some fruit trees. The fat fruit of the put (papaya) would be tasty, he thought to himself, and perhaps he would also plant a few avocado trees.

His eldest son was working another field to the south of town. He had seen him leave the family compound with his planting sack full of seed. They had collected the seed corn last night. Lahun's best corn from last year and that of his son had been mixed and shared. If one field of corn failed because of the harsh rains, the strong sun, or insect infestation, perhaps another field would flourish. His younger son had a field to the east, and in chac luum (red soil), he planted jicama *among the other crops. This hearty crop would add to the diet. Nearly all of the products from the* milpa *would be consumed by Lahun's family and the members of his sons' families.*

One section of Lahun's field was cut out of virgin forest. He began cutting the field in late summer and just before harvest in early fall. He chopped the big trees with his stone ax, felled them, girdled others, and cleared the bush. His two sons helped. Lahun was strong, but he was old. Cutting the forest made the young grow old very quickly because it was difficult and exhausting work. Part of his field was a milpa *that had been used the previous year, so clearing this section was easier. He cut the brush in the spring to dry it out. In the late spring, he fired the fields. The ash fertilized the thin soil. This year, the fields fired well— they were bone dry—and the rains held off until after the brush had burned.*

During the planting time, Lahun searched the sky hoping that the sun would pass away, that the clouds would come in, and that the mighty Chacob *would bring the rains needed to germinate his seeds. Lahun sat on a large stone to rest for a moment. He sat near the boundary of his field and the forest and looked into the forest, spotting the* buyluum, *a plant that grew only during the rainy season. The plant was no larger than his hand, but he had been taught by his grandfather to look for it. It marked the rainy season and, therefore, brought a smile to his face. Perhaps, it is the correct day to plant, he thought to himself. I must mention to my sons that I have seen* buyluum. *Perhaps, the rains will be favorable this year. I wonder if my sons have seen the plant to the south or to the east.*

Later, in the growing season, Lahun anxiously watched the sky as the rain clouds rolled in day after day but passed by his field. It was the u kin pek, *"the dog days," the* canicula, *or the* veranillo *(Hester 1954). With no rain for 10 days, his crop of maize was lost. Fortunately, his sons' fields to the south and east had been watered but only after a ceremony calling to the Rain Gods. People would suffer from the drought, Lahun thought, as they had in the years just before the* dzulob *(foreigners) arrived to stay in Tiho (Merida) and Saci (Valladolid) (Farriss 1984, Table 2.2). His family would survive because they had planted a* no-hoch col *(large* milpa) *and parts of it had been watered and would produce a good harvest. Working with his sons provided some security.*

Lahun remembered the earlier years when hideous diseases had swept the land. Disease had killed his parents, and he had lived with his father's brother. Later, when he was old enough to make milpa *and was newly married, the plague had destroyed the crops and disease had taken his beautiful, young wife and first son. His second wife was stronger than the first, and she knew how to use the medicinal plants that cured sicknesses. His sons were* milperos *now, and his daughter was ready for marriage.*

Lahun saw his wife coming along the path with his young daughter. His wife had a chu *(drinking gourd) hung over her shoulder (Figure 4.4). It surely contained water with honey or the rich* pozole *(corn gruel). His wife also carried a basket containing his midday meal, wrapped in cotton cloth, of good* gordas *(thick tortillas) prepared by his wife's own hand. He had forgotten his food in the morning rush to get to his* milpa. *He expected that his wife would bring the food and was glad to see her. She and his daughter were collecting* leña *(firewood) in*

Figure 4.4. Chuob *(water jugs) hung from the wall of a* chuyche *(pole-and-thatch house).*

the forest, and his daughter carried a small load of wood on her back with a tumpline across her forehead supporting the load. The three members of the family sat down to eat. Around them the wind blew gently through the forest, and the trees swayed slightly. His wife looked at the miserable corn with tears in her eyes. Lahun reassured her that the root crops in his field would survive the drought if the rains came soon and that the chile pepper planted near the house would be plenty for the family's needs. His younger daughter tended the chile plants near the house, and they were thriving. Perhaps, his wife's grief came from remembering the harsh years when families had suffered. Making a living under the forest canopy was hard work and uncertain, but with his eldest son to help him grow corn, jicama, fruit, and other crops, the family was secure—collective enterprise would ensure survival.

"GREEN GOLD" AND SUGARCANE: ECONOMIC BOOM AND BUST
(A.D. 1860–1915)

The Yucatan had little to offer the Spanish conquistadors, and thus, little interest in the peninsula was generated after it was occupied by the Montejos and other Spaniards in the mid-1500s. They reasoned that it was barely worth the struggle to conquer the Maya because the land was lacking in resources—there were no valuable metals, the soil was meager, production of grains was difficult, and the rains were fickle. Also, the insect pests were aggressive, malaria rampant, and the snakes deadly.

During the Mexican struggle for independence from Spain in the early 1800s, it was unclear whether the Yucatan would be incorporated into the new Mexican nation, whether the peninsula would secede and join Texas, or whether a request for annexation to the United States would be made. In the early 1800s, Yucatan was one of the poorest states in the new Mexican nation, but by 1830, Yucatecans had discovered "Green Gold", or henequen. By 1860, the Yucatecans had invented a defibration machine to accelerate production of henequen fiber. From 1880 to 1918, Yucatecans moved toward total commitment in the production of henequen for export, mainly to the United States (Baklanoff 1980; p. 208). Although machines were used to rasp and twine the fiber and small-gauge railroad spurs were used to transport it from field to processing and packing houses, the industry was still labor intensive. By 1910, most Yucatecan *campesinos* and servants were held in debt labor. The workers had a higher standard of living than workers elsewhere in Mexico, but they were tied tightly to the booming henequen plantations. By the turn of the century, Yucatan, which had been a dry and poor province, became a dry and rich province.

Henequen is native to the Yucatan and had been grown and processed since pre-Columbian times. It was well adapted to the arid lands of the northwest sector of the peninsula, and it was there that the plantations were built. They thrived, too, because of the Maya workers who were "attached" to the *hacendados* (hacienda owners).

To the south and east, the sugarcane industry developed. Unlike henequen, which was processed for export, cane sugar was produced almost entirely for internal consumption. Cane requires deeper soil than henequen and a more humid climate; therefore, its area of cultivation extended from the western portion of the peninsula south of Merida to the lands south of Valladolid into the interior of the peninsula (Wells 1985; p. 23). The sugarcane economy rapidly expanded after the War of Independence in 1810. Because of changes in the recognition of property rights, the communal lands of the Maya were appropriated by wealthy non-Indian entrepreneurs who set up sugarcane plantations.

By 1847, conditions on the peninsula, including the rise of the henequen industry, the power of plantation owners, the poverty of debt-servitude workers, and the eclipse of Indian communal lands in the interior by sugarcane magnates, exploded into war. The war was a social upheaval by the Maya to force the *dzulob* (foreigners) off the peninsula, and it was bloody and horrible. Estimates suggest that the population declined by 25 to 50% (Wells, 1985; p. 26). For two years, the battle raged, and the first truce was not signed until 1853. Although the sugar industry collapsed, the henequen industry continued and expanded in the northwest sector of the peninsula. In the west, the rich plantation owners built mansions and sent their children to schools in France. Merida, the "Green Gold" capital, became an urban center of the arts and culture. These riches were built on the backs of Maya workmen who lived and died on plantations working for the elite. However, on the frontier and beyond it to the east, the Maya lived much as they had lived centuries before the foreigners came (see Villa Rojas 1945).

THE VILLAGE OF KANXOC: 1860S

Francisco May had returned from his milpa *and was resting in his hammock in his home of poles and thatch. He had a long leaf of henequen in his arms and deliberately pulled fibers off the length of the leaf and twilled the strands into a longer piece across his thigh. This was the last leaf he would have to work. He had enough line to finish weaving the new hammock. He looked across the room and saw the two upright poles and the stretched henequen between them. A few more days and he would be finished with weaving. Next, he would weave a henequen bag to hold his seed at planting time. He could use the bark of the* hool *tree for a carrying strap on the bag. The bag would be easier to make than the hammock—smaller, less stitching. He rolled the fibers on his thigh to twill them. It was the wet season and he could see the thunderclouds building up for an afternoon downpour. His wife was bent over the clay* comal *making tortillas. She would slap the corn dough in her hands and lay the flattened cake on the griddle. It would sizzle, and its strong perfume would fill the room. The cake would puff up and look as if it were ready to float away. His wife would pinch the edge and flip the tortilla over and slap it flat. When the tortilla was cooked, she would gently put it in a gourd to keep it warm.*

He remembered when she had come to him as a young bride. She made the worst tortillas, half raw or half burned. She was young, could not cook, and was fearful of every night noise. She had changed in the last few years. Now she squatted by the fire working to prepare the daily meal. Her dress was bright white, embroidered with flowers around the yoke and at the hem. She had sewn

*the dress from fabric she had woven herself. He could see that she had begun
working on another dress. She had planted the cotton in the yard, watered it,
and picked the bolls. She had used the doughnut-shaped spindle whorl to make
thread and to weave the soft cotton mantle. Some of the threads used to embroider the dress she had dyed with plant concoctions (Figure 4.5). She was beautiful*

Figure 4.5. Huipil *design.*

in her old dress. His lovely wife was growing fat. In a few months, she would provide him with a child.

As Francisco May sat working, he was also thinking about his milpa, *beehives, henequen plants, and fruit trees. He had just purchased a young calf that he would fatten and later sell. With the cash, he would buy matches, coffee, sugar, and a new metal axe.*

His wife was working over the fire. She had wrapped some corn dough stuffed with venison in banana leaves and was boiling these tamales. She knew that her husband would enjoy eating them with some chile habanero *from her garden. She had prepared some tea by boiling the* yerbabuena *leaves. This would soothe his stomach, and the rains would not make him sick this year as it did to so many others in the village. She thought about her chickens and their chicks. Now, she had quite a few fowl and could begin to exchange eggs for other items that she needed (see Villa Rojas 1945).*

As a member of the Balam (Jaguar) family, she was very busy during the rainy season. The Balam women knew herbal remedies, and this was the time of sickness. She collected medicinal plants in the afternoon and noted where the important species were found. She was tired, and her back ached. In time, the aches would pass, and soon the baby would enter the world. Her mother would help when it was her time. She would squat to have the baby, and if there were pains, her mother would find plants and make medicine to reduce the pains.

Someone called out from the front yard, and her husband's brother, Bonifacio, walked through the door. He was a younger brother and, never satisfied to work in his fields, had moved to settle near Merida. There, he had worked on a henequen plantation, and it was a surprise to see him. He had aged in the few years since they had seen him. His breath was short, and he was wheezing. Francisco May asked if his brother wanted some warm herbal tea. His wife poured the aromatic liquid into a small lec *cup (half a small round gourd) and passed it to Bonifacio. He stared at the cup and lifted it to sip, saying not a word. Finally, he told them he had run from the Hacienda Yaxnic. He told of his work as a* jornalero de campo, *a field worker. The* hacendado *had given him a weekly wage, a small plot of land, a hut, firewood, water, and grazing land. At first, he had only a small debt, a* chan cuento, *to the hacienda store; but the debt started growing when he held his marriage ceremony and sponsored a fiesta. As the debt grew still larger, he tried to work harder. He cleared land, planted henequen, harvested it, and processed the fiber. However, his debt continued to grow, and finally, he bought less and less food from the company store. The poor diet weakened his wife, and she contracted* u kaxiltabal kik *(severe bloody diarrhea.) The* yerbatero *gave her vanilla powder in a tea made from a special vine, but she never recovered. Finally, when they had no more food, she became weaker and died.*

"I buried her, and it was as though I myself were buried. I wandered from job to job in a dream. I had no food, no family. The work was miserable. Finally, I just stayed in the hut. I stopped going to work. The overseer came to my hut and told me I had to get back to work. I sat there with my eyes cast down. He and another man brought me to a post and tied my hands to it. They beat and

whipped me until I fell to my knees. They shouted at me that in the morning I would work or they would whip me again. Then, they threw me into my hut. I lay moaning on my straw petate *(mat). My wife's sister came and cleansed my back of the blood. In the night, she half carried me to the edge of the hacienda. There, she passed me to her younger brother who carried me to a village where they hid me until I was strong enough to walk. I have been taken from the Hacienda Yaxnic and from village to village all the way here to Kanxoc. Bounty hunters are out there looking for me. I owe so much to the hacienda store, but I cannot go back; I will not go back.''*

Francisco looked at his younger brother covered with dust from his long trip. He took the warm water that his wife had heated for his bath and told his brother to follow him. They went off to a small bathing enclosure. When his brother removed his cotton tunic, Francisco's eyes filled with tears at what he saw. His brother's back was covered with scars, welts, and scabs. Gently, he poured the warm water over his younger brother's wounds.

The days, weeks, and months passed, and Francisco guarded the health and safety of his younger brother, Bonifacio. Rumors reached the village of Kanxoc of workers who escaped slavery on the henequen plantations or of sporadic violence that was crushed by the Guardia Nacional *(National Guard). The elite lived in constant fear of an Indian uprising.*

To the south of Kanxoc in Peto, the sugarcane plantation owners were taking more *ejidal* (common) lands and pressing the native population into service. The *dzulob* encroached on Indian lands, and the laws limited the mobility of the *campesino* (native agriculturalist). The work regimen on the plantations altered the traditional Maya way of life, and the migration of Yucatecans into the southeast led to an explosive social situation. The pressures on production, changes in the organization of work or economic life and in the techniques of production, and control over land led to fighting, starvation, and disease. War, with all of its hideous components, exploded on the peninsula.

Francisco May relaxed and watched his son pile the firewood near the hearth. His son, Silvestre May Balam, was 10 years old now. The child was strong and healthy and was beginning to work with him and his uncle, Bonifacio, making milpa. *The boy was able to cut small saplings and could plant seed. He was able to weed and helped stack corn at harvest time. He was a gentle boy, kind to his uncle who never quite regained his strength or sanity after returning from the Hacienda Yaxnic. This was a toublesome time, Francisco thought. To the south, there were skirmishes between the Indians and the cane hacienda owners. To the east, the* Guardia Nacional *and bounty hunters were hunting Indians that had run from servitude. Francisco relaxed and rasped fiber off of a henequen leaf. He would make a seed bag for for his brother to use. His brother had refused to work with the fiber; but that's all right, thought Francisco. His brother tended the bees, and that was a good thing. The bees seemed to produce rich honey when Bonifacio brought the hives in from the forest. He was keen on locating the nests of workers and competent in transporting them through the forest at night to the racks near the house. He tended the bees, organized the U-hanli-cab (the ceremony to protect the hives), and built additional racks to hold the tree trunks. Francisco had bad luck with the bees: They escaped, died, or produced sour honey when he tried to work with them. Now he could stay away and let his brother take care of them. Francisco could plant more fruit trees. He was putting in another banana grove, had planted avocado and papaya saplings in his* milpa, *and was cutting the* ramon *tree branches to feed his cattle. His wife tended the chickens and the pigs. She worked on the small garden plots near the house. The rains had been good for two years now, and Francisco had a store of three years of maize. Life under the tropical canopy seemed to be good.*

As Francisco continued working, a shadow appeared in the doorway. There stood his elder brother, Teodosio May. His brother lived in a village near Tepich. He was a milpero. *As his brother entered the room, Francisco saw that the front of his tunic was covered with blood. Dried blood flaked off his hands. "The white men, women, and children of Tepich have been slaughtered, and some of the young girls were raped," Teodosio told Francisco.*

Kanxoc was located on the frontier between the rich haciendas of the northwest sector of Yucatan and the poor, Indian villages of the southeast. In Kanxoc, where the Indian population practiced traditional economic strategies to survive and where sons, daughters, brothers, and fathers migrated out of the villages to work as wage laborers on haciendas, the struggle toward modernization would be born. This birth, as is true for all births, would begin in pain and in blood.

THE MODERN ECONOMY

Silvestre May Balam sat in his father's house. He had been taught to live and work in the forest. His first responsibility was to make milpa. *Throughout the year, he attended to the land. The forest needed to be slashed back, the brush dried and pulled to the sides of the* col, *or* milpa, *to make a high fence, or* sop', *to protect the field from the wandering cattle. The brush needed to be fired and the seed planted in the rich ash. The field needed to be walked over with a digging stick, and the pockets of soil planted with corn and bean seed. Squash seed was also planted, and the large-leafed plant kept the weeds down. The field needed to be weeded with a machete or a* coa *(curved knife.) With sufficient rain, but not too much, without insect plague or attacks by vermin, and after four full moons had passed, the corn would be ripe and ready for harvesting. Fruit-bearing saplings and banana groves were planted. Honey was collected or sugarcane was planted for a sweetener. Chickens and turkeys were kept near the house. A few pigs, some cattle, perhaps a horse or two, or a mule were bought in the good years, sold or slaughtered in the bad years. His young wife tended to the household, cooked the meals, sewed and cleaned the clothes, cultivated gardens adjacent to the house, wove hammocks, and practiced other crafts.*

Kanxoc was growing as a village, and families were beginning to move away. The farmland was being used up. The high rainforest areas were being cut down. Harvests were not as rich as they were in the years of his father and his father's brothers. The game near Kanxoc was scarce, only a few deer, and fewer wild pig, roaming the forest. The wild birds had been reduced in number, and Silvestre May wandered farther and farther from the village seeking game and fertile lands. He was friendly with men in the town who migrated during the rainy season across the boundary of the state of Yucatan into the territory of Quintana Roo. In Quintana Roo in the east of the peninsula, the most traditional Maya villages were found, and Indian rebels from the Caste War that was fought during his father's generation lived in the forest. These Indians, the Cruzob, were never controlled by the national or state government. The territory was a refuge region (Aguirre Beltran 1979), with little foreign intrusion. Many of the Kanxoc milperos migrated to the east in June, at the beginning of the rainy season. They joined camps to cut the zapote trees and collect chicle (the latex gum resin), which was boiled, set up in marquetas (blocks), and sold to merchants. The cash income was then used to purchase items for the family household such as sugar and matches. This year Silvestre May and his brothers were going into the territory to collect chicle and hunt. One area where a chicle camp had been operating was along the shores of a small series of lakes. He would head there with his brothers. One of the lakes was called Lake Coba.

By the time Silvestre May Balam moved with his family to Coba in the 1950s, the pattern of economic life under the tropical canopy was fixed but flexible. It was adjusted to the limitations, constraints, and possibilities of the resources of the natural world and of the organization of social networks within and beyond the village boundaries. Although corn was central to the economic livelihood of the Maya, it was never a dependable staple. From 1975 to 1985 in Coba, only two good productive years were reported. During that decade, there were two years when the harvest produced only half of what it should have and six years when the harvest was lost—a crop failure rate of four years out of five.

Though it is an undependable and labor intensive investment, the cultivation of corn by the Maya has been the focus of Maya life and of investigations by scholars. The probable reason for its importance is that it is capital free. Maya villagers may have access to a growing labor force within the growing family, but they have little or no cash. Corn not only supplies bulk and calories to the diet, but with beans and chile peppers, it helps to provide protein and essential vitamins and, in a gruel with honey, it supplies quick energy. These are basically capital free although intensive labor is necessary in cultivating a *milpa* plot or in building and cultivating a kitchen garden.

To offset the economic failure of corn cultivation and harvest, the Maya have traditionally cultivated fruit and nut trees (Folan, Fletcher, and Kintz 1979) or relied on wild trees. Citrus fruit trees are favored, and these include sour orange, lemon, and lime. The sour orange tree is hardy and, once established, is tolerant of drought. Its branches will also take grafts of the more valued mandarin orange. Papaya and avocado trees also supplement the Maya diet with tasty, calorie- and vitamin-rich fruits. Banana groves are cultivated either in the yard area or in special orchards in the forest. The banana is small and sweet and used to relieve diarrhea, a common ailment among the Maya, especially during the rainy season.

In ancient and modern times, apiculture, or beekeeping, has been an important industry in Yucatan. Nowadays, the traditional *colecab* (stingless bee) varieties that were housed in tree trunks have been replaced by North American honeybees housed in boxlike hives. The honey of the *colecab* is watery but sweet and deposited in round sacklike holders. The North American bees are more productive, but their disadvantage is that they sting. Some remote ranchos still stack the *colecab,* but sadly, the *colecab* are dying out and are no longer kept in the village of Coba. Apiculture can provide a family with sufficient work and cash so that work in the *milpa* can be abandoned. This is the case with one of the relatively wealthy men in Coba, Daniel Cen. He was the first to purchase hives of the stinging honeybees and has made part of his fortune selling honey. Although as a young man, he did cultivate *milpa,* he no longer needs to in order to support his family.

Women plant herbs, tomatoes, chiles, onions, garlic, tobacco, and other condiments around their houses to supplement the diet of their own families. They can also sell their surplus and use this income for minor purchases in the village stores or exchange garden products within the extended family and among close friends. Not all families grow all the possible crops; thus, the minor foods are distributed by exchange or by retailing at a few pesos here and there. Some of the women have been taught the medicinal qualities of the garden plants—the herbal remedies that protect the health of their spouses and children—and they cultivate these in their kitchen gardens. For example, *yerbabuena* is brewed as a tea to calm an upset stomach. The women also raise domestic animals, such as chickens, turkeys, and pigs. These resources are used to satisfy subsistence needs, social obligations, and ritual requirements (Pohl and Feldman, 1982).

Members of the family practice assorted handicrafts, supplying their own needs or sometimes selling their products. Handicrafts can provide a good income. One family in Coba has several sewing machines and produces *huipiles* (Figure 4.6). These sell at a high price and are desired items. Several of the women sell *huipiles* to tourists. There is one tailor in town. Other handicrafts produced in town include woven hammocks, small wooden seats, and baskets. One man in town is a carpenter, and several men are masons. These activities to a lesser or greater extent supplement a family's household budget.

A few individuals operate stores, restaurants, and *artesanias* (handicraft stores) catering to the new tourist industry. Local families buy eggs, tomatoes, coffee, cookies, cigarettes, and chewing gum, in the local stores. They can also find shirts or pants, polyester dresses, shoes, laundry soap and bleach, notebooks for the children to use in school, paper, envelopes, pens, and pencils. A few restaurants operate in the village, serving *huevos rancheros*, or ranch-style eggs, with *tortillas* or white bread, chicken and rice soup, sandwiches, venison steak or stew, pork, beef, rice, potatoes, and salads. You can sip a soft drink, a beer, or a lemonade. The artisan shops mostly ca-

Figure 4.6. Young girl in a huipil *sewn by her mother.*

ter to the tourists and sell them traditional *huipiles*, black coral, T-shirts with
bird motifs (a toucan or a parrot), and cold soft drinks.

The economic system of the *Cobaeños* is modern. Although families and
friends still barter goods and the religious festivals collect food and redistrib-

ute it, the modern Maya purchase goods for their households priced according to supply and demand. To satisfy the economic needs of the family, the men and women of modern Coba have plunged into the wage labor stream. This provides cash but strains social ties. When the jobs for men are out of town, on the coast of Quintana Roo in construction or in various parts of the peninsula in archaeology, the men go off as they did when cutting *chicle* when Quintana Roo was a major gum supplier. To understand how easily the Maya have been able to enter the wage labor stream, it is important to gain a picture of the past and project it into the future.

During the pre-Columbian period, the Maya agriculturalist paid tax or tribute to the Maya Lords. The payment was corn, cacao, or other food-stuffs, cotton fabric, pottery, or labor (Roys 1931). However, the organization of distribution in the pre-Columbian capitals was such that the workers contributed their goods to the *batab* (ruler), and the lords redistributed goods from their storehouses in times of great need. When the Spaniards entered the peninsula to stay in the 1550s, the *estancias*, or Spanish cattle ranches, although modest in comparison to ranches in other parts of New Spain, attached Indians to them who worked for the owners. During this Colonial period, the Indian owed tribute to the Spanish, under the *encomienda* system. The Indians were also forced to pay the clergy alms; there were civil levies to support Indian courts and fees for baptism, marriage, wills, and funerals. There were community taxes and head taxes. The *repartimiento* system was also instituted during the Colonial period. It was a system of production quotas imposed on the native population. At times the quotas were so excessive that they interferred with food production.

During the henequen boom in the northwest sector of the Yucatan and during the development of sugarcane plantations in the nineteenth and early twentieth centuries, the Maya were attached to *haciendas* by debt peonage and were virtually slaves working for the elite. This was not something new, for a hierarchy of the rich and powerful and the poor and powerless had endured as a system since the ancient Maya civilization arose in the peninsula.

Although the *campesinos* were paid wages while working on the henequen haciendas, the company store indebted them to the owner to such an extent that an independent existence was impossible. The possibility of a more independent and profitable existence for the Maya did, however, exist on the frontier. As far back as early records show, the Maya have always moved from zone to zone, and they continue to migrate in modern times.

During the Colonial period, the Maya moved into the forest when the tax and tribute or other demands of the Spanish colonial administration became harsh and unbearable. The Maya disappeared into the forest with their families where they were able to eke out a living under the tropical canopy.

During the nineteenth and early twentieth centuries, when rebellion was in the air in Mexico, the Maya politically controlled the east sector of the peninsula and continued traditional strategies of economic adaptation to the difficult landscape. Many of the Maya were able to reject the demeaning economic poverty and punishment of debt peonage on the henequen and sugar haciendas and escape into the eastern territory of Quintana Roo.

In the 1920s, *chicle* production boomed, and the Maya in the eastern sector of the peninsula were able to cut *chicle* and maintain their agricultural cycle, arboriculture, and apiculture. This mixed economy was perhaps the best mode to ensure survival.

The men worked in camps during the rainy season, cutting the zapote trees, gathering the *chicle* gum, boiling it in copper cauldrons, and pressing it into molds to cool. Sometimes, men put rocks or *masa* (corn dough) inside the *chicle* blocks before selling them. The work paid well but was dangerous.

Stories were told of spirits that ranged through the camps. When a *chiclero* died in the camps, his body was buried there, and the man's spirit was said to haunt the place. When a man climbed a *zapote* tree and cut a zig-zagged line to let the sap run into bags at the bottom of the trunk, if he was not alert, he would accidently cut his rope and not the trunk and sometimes fall to his death.

In the past as in the present, the Maya agriculturalist could only rarely produce all he and his family needed to survive. Wage labor was an additional task to ensure the family's welfare; however, it did alienate the Maya from the products of his labor. In the past, the Maya were peasants or craftsmen, giving services or produce to the Lords in the town and getting services in return—from those who were responsible for the collective welfare of the community. Now, the Maya constitute a rural proletariat whose labor can be bought and sold.

ECONOMIC POTENTIAL

The corn-based economy provides a narrow margin of safety for the Maya. The Maya, like the Zapotec studied by Kearney (1972, p. 8), have found that crop failure leads to debt or forces them to migrate out for temporary or seasonal work. Living on the economic knife blade, the Maya have small opportunity for capital accumulation. The Maya, like rural farmers all over Latin America, consume 70% to 90% of what they produce within the family as subsistence-level goods (Nelson 1973, p. 24). Wages are low and are used to fulfill subsistence-level needs. The number of households that cannot earn a living from farming a parcel of land is high, and arboriculture, apiculture, animal husbandry, and wage labor are essential activities to ensure a livelihood. The Maya, well aware of the limits of corn farming, have a long history of diversifying their economic activities. Successful farming in the Maya area entails investing in low-risk endeavors, low-cost projects, and products adapted to a local microenvironment. The Maya have been characterized as "conservative" for these values; however, living at risk has promoted a safety-first principle in adapting to the tropical environment. Intensive and alternative agricultural possibilities have been practiced by the

Maya to diminish the impact of frequent crop failure. Intensive dooryard gardening, planting in dry cenotes, and planting orchards reduce the risk of starvation.

Beginning with the 1910 Revolution, the core and the heart of Mexico's rural reform to alleviate rural starvation, poverty, and powerlessness has been the organization of the *ejido* where rural farmers have been given access to lands by the federal government. According to Simpson (1937, p. 481), however, "full circle turns the wheel"—peons into communists, peasants into *ejiditarios,* communists into individuals—*ejiditarios* into capitalists." Economy and politics (power) merge.

5/Political Leadership

Among the Maya, the political organization has been and remains very complex. Before the invasion by the Spanish, the Maya were periodically organized in city-states that subsequently collapsed only to be reorganized once again. The Maya reorganized at Chichen Itza, which later fell as a center of power. They reorganized at Mayapan, and this center of power also fell. The Maya again organized into small city-states, but these collapsed when the Spanish conquistadors entered the peninsula and eventually gained control of substantial portions of the land and its resources. The political centers suffered again in the mid-1800s. Much of the political struggle in the Yucatan was over access to land and labor. The pre-Columbian society was divided into ruling elite, middle-class artisans, and subservient commoners (Figure 5.1). After the arrival of the Spanish conquistadors, the divisive classes within the society were the ruling foreigners and the indigenous Maya.

ITZAM NA: IGUANA HOUSE OF POWER AND SACRIFICE (A.D. 600–900)

The people had gathered in front of the large pyramid located in the center of Coba. For a uinal (20 days), the ruler and his wife had not been seen. The royal pair had been separated, never seeking each other, celibate, approached only by their priestly attendants. Having fasted for the upcoming ceremony, they were brought to the temples to be sequestered for the final five days.

When the days of fasting ended, the woman was carried to the temple, and the bloodletting ceremonies began. She had her ears pierced with the tail spine of a stingray, and the attendants caught her blood in strips of cloth. The cloths were burned and the smoke consumed by the gods (Schele and Miller 1986, p. 80). She chanted to Ix Chebel Yax, *patroness of Coba. She collected her own blood and made her own marks to the "Lady Unique of the Painted Brushes" and the "Lady Unique Owner of the Cloth"—manifestations of* Ix Chebel Yax. *With her own red blood, she painted red lines on the floor of the temple. She became the Goddess Weaver, the Creator Goddess, and Mistress of Earth—other manifestations.* Ix Chebel Yax *was also the Rain Goddess, and her husband, Itzam Na was the Rain God (Thompson 1970, p. 206). Her attendants supported her as she sat on the rush pallet. She was queen of Coba, and she became* Ix

Figure 5.1. The power of the rulers of the Maya as represented in a Jaina figurine.

Chebel Yax. *The vision of the goddess appeared to her, and she entered the vision. She saw her husband,* Itzam Na, *the Creator God. Slowly, they lifted her. It was time.*

Covered with a red cotton cloak and a headdress of red woodpecker feathers, the beautiful Creator Goddess was half carried out into the sun to be viewed by the people of Coba. They swayed to the tunkel *drum beat as she was led out of the dark cave of the temple into the brilliant sunlight. The people chanted softly,* "Ix Chebel Yax, Ix Chebel Yax," *and she looked down upon them—this Mistress of the Earth. She was weak after the fasting and bloodletting, and she had become transformed. Slowly, the attendants turned her toward the other palace temple, and she saw her husband,* Itzam Na. *He also was being carried by his attendants. Across his shoulder was a cloak of blue cotton, the special color of the Rain God,* Itzam Na Kauil *or "Iguana House Bountiful Harvest." Near his side was the* Chac Itzam Na, *his brother, with the red cloak symbolizing east, and* Sac Itzam Na, *his uncle, wearing the white cloak symbolizing north. At his feet,* Ek Itzam Na, *his youngest son, was wrapped with the black cloak symbolizing west. The priest* Ah Kin, *the diviner, and* Ah Nacom, *the sacrificer, stood by his side (Thompson 1970).* Itzam Na, *"He Who Dwelt in the Sky," stood in the center, and behind him on the horizon the clouds were rolling in and bringing rain. The crowd saw the clouds, trembled to the drum beat, and chanted,* Ix Chebel Yax" *and* "Itzam Na." *The priestly attendants brought the blood cloths to the front of the temples and, placing them in stone containers, set them on fire. The smoke rose in front of* Itzam Na, *covering him in the cloud, and he walked forward to stand by his wife. Through fasting and sacrifice, the royal pair had created a vision of themselves as god and goddess. They brought the rain, and they created the world, weaving its pattern. Through the transformation, they held power over the crowd.*

In the crowd stood the costume maker and his son. The two softly chanted, "Ix Chebel Yax" *and* "Itzam Na" *to the drum beat. The old costume maker looked at the temples where he saw the young dancers in costumes he had painstakingly created. The dancers headdresses were stuffed with iguana skins emerging from the front symbolizing* Itzam Na *or "Iguana House." A few dancers had ear ornaments of bird bone symbolizing the sky. They all wore jade pendants, the sacred blue-green stone, which was the special color of the Rain God,* Itzam Na. *They all wore white loinclothes splattered with blood because the dancers had performed the bloodletting ritual (Schele and Miller 1986, p. 193). The old man looked at the beautiful* Ix Chebel Yax. *"Ix Chebel Yax," he prayed softly, "Mistress of the Earth, please send the rains to us." Squatting down, the old man perforated his tongue and sacrificed his own blood. The crowd focused on* Itzam Na *and* Ix Chebel Yax, *the bearers of the most powerful blood among them all. Through the bloodletting sacrifice of the Lord and his Mistress, the god and his consort were born, and these powers came into the life of the Maya.*

That very night far from the center of town a man lay awake near his sleeping wife on a straw mat. The home was modestly built of pole and thatch. The man lay listening to the rain fall on his roof. In the darkness, he remembered his wife's offering of a little blood from her earlobe. He silently rose up, and taking five kernels of blue corn, he walked to the doorway. Whispering "Itzam Na," he threw the blue kernels out into the rain, and they were absorbed into the cavelike darkness.

THE ITZA "WATER WITCH" HOUSE (A.D. 900–1200)

The center of Coba was set on an elevated platform marking the sacred center of the city and distinguishing it from the secular periphery. Here, pyramid structures, temples, palaces, residences of the Lords of Coba and their attendants, and some priests' dwellings were found. The center of the city had hidden altars and areas where access was restricted by entry through narrow alleyways and up narrow staircases (Folan, Kintz, and Fletcher 1983). The center of the city had been built at the command of the Lords of Coba and the priests. They had organized the town's labor forces to construct and enlarge the pyramids.

The Lord of Coba called the stone cutters who were working on the new temple to musencab *into the plaza* (Figure 5.2). *Through the* Chilam Balam *(Jaguar Speaker), he addressed them. "You will gather together all of the men in your section and bring them to work with you tomorrow. All of the men must work to complete the monument and to drag the carved stone monuments of our ancestors to be positioned in the temple at the base of the pyramid. The men will work*

Figure 5.2. Noboch Mul, dedicated to Musencab, Coba.

for me until the temple is finished. Bring all the men to work. There is no harvest this year, the season has been dry. Families are hungry. Bring the men to build the temple, and I will give them corn from my storage houses. All of the men must come and work on the temple. If they are sick, they still must come. I will feed them from my storehouse and feed their families. Bring all the h-men *to the center of the city, and they will pray for the sick and cure them.''*

The Lord of Coba looked at his subjects. The years were dry and barren, and the cheeks of his people were caving in. ''How long will it be,'' he wondered, ''how long will we suffer, how long until we have a harvest again?'' His stores would feed the city only a few years. Although the city provided quantities of honey and traded it to city-states in the west and to the south, the people were weak with hunger from the ongoing drought. He was suffering from his worries over the Itza's demand for tribute. The warriors of the Lord of Coba had forced the Itza back, but they had an economic stranglehold on the territory (see Andrews and Robles 1985, pp. 62–72). His power to protect his people was slipping away.

COCOM HOUSE AT MAYAPAN (A.D. 1283–1441)

With the passing of time, the Itza hegemony at Chichen Itza ended, and the city of Mayapan was founded in the *katun* 13 *Ahau* (1263–1283) (see Pollock et al. 1962; Bricker 1981, p. 26; Edmunson 1982, pp. xvi, 16, 89). It was at that time that the Xiu, Canul, and Cocom families established a joint government at Mayapan. The Cocom family ruled under the Itza legacy, and it was a time of debauchery, terror, and war. Rulers governed like beasts of prey, resorted to sorcery, and according to legend, turned themselves into foxes or lynxes *(ch'amac)*. It was a time when the *uaay*, animal spirits of evil sorcerers, stalked people.

The Cocom ruler stood in front of the Temple to Kukulcan, *the ''Feathered Serpent,'' at Mayapan. He looked at the building and knew that it was a small and shoddy replication of the larger Temple to* Kukulcan *at Chichen Itza to the east. ''The stone carvers are imbeciles,'' he muttered to himself. He walked using a staff, symbol of his power, but he was leaning more heavily on it than in previous years. He entered his residence, and there he saw two of his many concubines, younger women born into a subordinate lineage. The cult of the* nicte *or* plumeria *flower allowed him to take multiple wives or consorts. He had little shame in taking any women offered to the royal household.*

The ruler was waiting for the head of his guard, Ah Paal Canul, to appear before him. The Canul family warriors stood at their stations along the wall to protect the city of Mayapan. There was word of dissent among the other ruling families and whispers of treachery among the Tutul Xiu family.

The Cocom ruler relaxed on his royal pallet waiting for the announcement of the arrival of his guard. He thought briefly of his son, Nachi Cocom, who was heading a trading expedition to the south. In the south, his son would trade slaves for jade, shell beads, and metal objects.

The ruler signaled his attendants to cover his shoulders with a quetzal-feather cloak. He toyed with the jade beads around his neck and twirled the jade earplugs hanging to his shoulder. Nervously, he awaited the arrival of the guard. His concubines sat on jaguar pelts and wove cotton. Their long hair curled down their backs like the coils of a serpent. They glanced in his direction, and he saw their blood-red spondylus pendants and beaded necklace.

The attendants slipped through the door of the domicile to announce the arrival of the Canul guard. Ah Paal Canul stepped through the doorway to greet his Lord. Falling to his knees, he murmured, and crawled toward the Lord. Raising his body, he pulled a stingray spine from his cloak and leaped on the Cocom ruler and stabbed him through the eye with the dart. The ruler shuddered and screamed, and Ah Paal Canul pulled out a knife and slit his own throat.

Quickly, the room filled with Canul, Xiu, and Ah Kin Chel traitors. The consorts were terrified, but their screams were quickly silenced, and their blood flowed onto the stone floor, finally reaching the blood line of their husband and the blood of the Canul guard.

The sign of Kukulcan had been erased, the blue-green feather-cloaked ruler was gone from his throne, the Red Earth symbols of the spondylus were no longer breathing on the breasts of the women. The Maya symbols of power were drenched in blood, washed away, and the peninsula floundered again in political chaos.

THE COCOM AT SOTUTA (A.D. 1441–1511)

When Nachi Cocom returned to Mayapan and learned of the slaughter of his family, he gathered his followers, and they walked to the east. First, they reached Tibolon and settled there. Shortly, they moved to Sotuta (see Roys 1962, p. 59; Tozzer 1941, Notes 216, 217). To the west lived the hated Xiu, and the territory of the Canul was on the northwestern shore. To the north, the territory of the Chels extended to the salt fields by the sea.

Nachi Cocom became a ferocious *nacom* or war leader partly because of his training as a trader/warrior and partly because of his reaction to the murder of his family at Mayapan. He relived the story of the blood bath in the palace of his father in his dreams and was constantly involved in purification ritual, fasting, and bloodletting, seeking a vision of his dead father, the priest-ruler-god, Kukulcan, or the ruler Cocom. South of the capital of the independent Cocom state of Sotuta were the towns of Kanchunup, Xiat, Popox, Uayacuz, and Tekom. Nachi Cocom would travel through this territory and walk through these towns that had *kancab* (red earth mortar) facing the buildings. Obsessed, the ruler would hold bloodletting ceremonies over the red earth. The area became populated with native religious practitioners who continued the practice of human sacrifice by depositing bodies in cenotes whence the dead would enter the Underworld (Roys 1957).

THE HOUSE OF ARMOR AND THE CROSS (A.D. 1511–1812)

The cyclical nature of time gave the Maya profound faith in the predictions of priests with respect to happenings in the next cycle round (Edmunson 1982, p. xi). The predictions were made by Jaguar Prophets, or *Chilam Balam*.

The cycles of time, or katun cycles, were set or seated by particular cities that then assumed dynastic and religious primacy over the whole peninsula for 13 *katuns* of 20 years each. At the end of this period, the city and all of its roads and idols were ritually destroyed, and a new seat of power was established at the beginning of a new *katun* cycle. The Itza seated a new *katun* cycle in 6 *Ahau* (948–968) at Champoton, and later, they seated another *katun* cycle at Chichen Itza. In 2 *Ahau,* the Xiu of Uxmal and Itza (Cocom) of Chichen Itza compromised and seated the *katun* cycle at Mayapan, which was centrally located and, for a time, jointly ruled. When the cycle came around again (8 *Ahau*) in 1441, the reign of power at Mayapan was over. The seating of the *katun* cycle in the years 1461–1539 was claimed by Chichen Itza, Izamal, Uxmal, Tihosuco, Emal, and Coba.

In 1511, the members of the House of Armor and the Christian Cross were shipwrecked on the east coast of the Yucatan peninsula. Two Spaniards, Geronimo de Aguilar and Gonzalo Guerrero, survived. Aguilar would later be found by Hernando Cortés and accompany him to the Valley of Mexico to participate in the conquest of the mighty Mexica (Aztec). Gonzalo Guerrero had adopted the Maya way of life, taken a Maya wife, risen high in Maya society, and refused to join Cortes's expedition (see Chamberlain 1966, p. 15).

After the first contact in 1511 and the second exposure in 1519 to Cortés's expedition, the Maya remained isolated from the Spanish presence until Francisco de Montejo the Father initiated his first campaign to conquer Yucatan in 1527. He entered the peninsula from the eastern shore and was graciously received on the island of Cozumel. However, his army was attacked at Chauaca and Ake as he marched west. Forced back to the coast, Montejo sailed to Spain in 1529 to petition for supplies. He was delayed in the mother country until the 1540s (see Chamberlain 1966, pp. 35–66), but his son would lead the next expedition.

The second campaign to conquer Yucatan began in 1531 and lasted only three years. Because the east coast was far too isolated for a campaign beginning there to succeed, the Spaniards under Montejo the Younger, the illegitimate son of Francisco de Montejo, moved onto the Yucatan peninsula from the southwest coast (see Chamberlain 1966, pp. 69–98, 132–149). Montejo the Younger moved through the Tabasco lowlands and onto the Yucatan peninsula, founding a center of military operation at Campeche. He had been instructed by his father to march north, to move into the north-central area of Yucatan, and to subjugate the native *caciques* (rulers) and their subjects. The north and north-central areas were the most populous most warlike, and most powerful in the Yucatan. The message from father to son was to apply the principle of divide and conquer, play one Maya state against another, and aggravate already existing hatreds and rivalries.

The Spaniards finally reached Chichen Itza, with its ball court, temples, and palaces in ruins, and used this rubble to build a Spanish city. Here were cenotes providing an inexhaustible source of water. Ancient Chichen, the capital of the Itza and the center of the sacred cult of worship focused on *Kukulcan,* became a Spanish center named Ciudad Real de Chichen Itza. Nacon Cupul, *cacique* of the nearby pueblo of Chichen, ordered his subjects to aid in the construction of temporary pole-and-thatch buildings to house Montejo and his troops. Although the Cupul lords gave obedience to the Spaniards and appeared to acquiesce to the overlordship of the castellaños, events were to prove that independence from the foreign intruders was the true state of the Maya mind. The Cupul of Chichen Itza seemed to accept the Spaniards, but Cupul *caciques* in the surrounding area were resentful. The Xiu to the west were staunch allies of the Spaniards mostly because of their hatred and animosity toward the Cocom of Sotuta. It is certainly unlikely that any Cocom *cacique* of Sotuta province gave allegiance to the Spaniards. Also, it is doubtful that the great Cupul religious, military, and political center of Saci (later to be named "Valladolid" by the Spaniards) gave their allegiance to the invaders. The Cupul lords were proud, warlike, and independence loving, and they never intended to permit the Spaniards to live among them permanently. Saci, the Cupul capital had one of the most beautiful cenotes on the peninsula and was the home of the powerful and feared war chief Nacahun Noh (Roys 1957). In 1533 the Cupul attacked the Spanish enclave at Chichen Itza. Although the attack failed, the Maya blockaded the town for a few months and forced the Spaniards to retreat to Campeche.

(Oblivious to the deep resentment that the Maya lords and their subjects had for the foreign intrusion, the Spaniards permitted the trusted native leaders of the Cupul to walk among them. In the Spanish headquarters at Ciudad Real de Chichen Itza, Francisco de Montejo the Younger admitted the Cupul Lord, Nacon Cupul, to his living quarters. Montejo talked of tribute, labor service, religious conversion, and of how the *caciques* should receive the Spanish conquistadors in peace as loyal vassals and servants of his Majesty the King of Spain. He spoke of tribute, of how much maize, beans, honey, wax, turkey, cotton, and pottery should be given. Nacon Cupul, High Lord and Priest of the Maya of Chichen Itza, glanced at the Spanish leader relaxed in his headquarters. Montejo had no idea of the hatred mounting among the Maya, and when he turned his back on the Maya Lord and mumbled more about tribute and labor drafts, the long pent-up hostility burst forth. Nacom Cupul pulled Montejo's sword from its sheath and tried to drive the blade into the enemy's backside. Montejo screamed, and a Spanish soldier rushed forward and cut off the arm of Nacon Cupul. Other soldiers rushed into the room and slaughtered the Maya Lord. As a result of this murder, the Maya subjects rose up in rebellion but the revolt was put down only to smolder. The Cupul towns refused to provide any tribute. The services that the Spaniards demanded and depended on to live in Ciudad Real de Chichen Itza were cut off. Food supplies were growing low, and Montejo the Younger sent soldiers out to the pueblos to seize supplies. The Cupul resisted, threw up barricades to defend themselves, and sent warriors out to cut off, trap, and slaughter the Spaniards.)

The Cupul realized the vulnerability of the Spanish position at Ciudad Real. The Spaniards were located far inland and could readily be isolated. They could be supplied by the other Spanish encampments only with difficulty and were heavily dependent on the native population for food. The Cupul could defend their pueblos against the weakened Spanish soldiers, confine the Spaniards to the town, and threaten them with starvation.

In the middle of 1533, the Cupul moved against the Spaniards with open warfare. By combining the forces of the great *caciques* and priests of Saci and the great Cupul military and religious leaders, the powerful and feared war chief of Saci, Nacahun Noh, led his warriors against Ciudad Real in a hot wave of hatred. Spaniards and their Indian slaves were slaughtered, and horses were destroyed. The Spanish settlement was blockaded.

In the Maya camp around the Spanish settlement of Ciudad Real sat the Cupul *nacom,* Nacahun Noh. To his side sat Nachi Cocom, Lord of the Sotuta province. The struggle between the Spanish conquistadors and the Maya Lords for control over the land of the Maya had begun. Months passed, the blockade held, and the position of the Spanish soldiers deteriorated. Perishing from hunger and dying slowly at the hands of the enemy, the Spaniards resolved to die valiantly fighting in battle. In late winter of 1533 or early spring of 1534, the Spanish soldiers sallied forth, attacking the Maya with all their forces. The Maya numbers overwhelmed them, the strong Maya fortifications held, and the Spaniards retreated with crippling losses.

The Spaniards made plans to retreat by slipping through the Maya supply lines running to the north coast where they would find their Maya allies, the Cehpech and Ah Kin Chel. From there, they could rejoin other Spanish troops. Under the cover of night, they slipped through the enemy's lines and began the rapid march to the north. At daybreak, the Maya discovered the ruse and began a furious pursuit. However, the Spaniards were able to escape and the Maya returned to their homeland in victory, rid of the intruders. Montejo the Father returned from Spain, was reunited with his son, and immediately began planning to reenter the Maya interior; but from the time that the Spaniards abandoned their attempts to conquer the Maya in the year 1534 until the founding of Merida in 1542, the eastern Maya lived free from the heavy yoke of Castilian political control.

From 1535 to 1541, the peninsula suffered severe famine due to drought and locust plagues (Farriss 1984, p. 61; Chamberlain, pp. 202–203; Tozzer 1941, pp. 54–55). The rains failed to water the crops, and starvation was so severe that men dropped dead in the streets. Finally, the Xiu of the western province petitioned the Cocom of the eastern province for safe passage through their territory to travel to Chichen Itza to the *Cenote Sagrado* (''Sacred Cenote'') to sacrifice idols and slaves. Sacrifices would be made by the

"Rain Bringer," Napot Xiu. The Cocom agreed to the passage and housed the enemy Xiu in a large residence in the Cocom settlement of Otzmal. When the "Rain Bringer," Xiu *batabs* (governors), and their attendants had retired for the night, the Cocom set the house on fire and killed all who tried to escape. In the night, the red flames reached the sky, and the agonized screams of the victims were heard. Nachi Cocom, descendant of the ruler of Mayapan who had been murdered by the Xiu, Canul, and Ah Kin Chel conspirators, sought revenge by setting on fire the great house filled with the Xiu. In addition to those burned to death, forty *principales* (important men) from the Xiu town of Mani, capital of their province, were murdered. Nachi Cocom had plotted to kill them, ordered them killed, their heads cut off, their eyes put out, and their tongues removed. Nachi Cocom ordered this murder because the Xiu nobles permitted the Spaniards to enter the country from the west, receiving the Spaniards in peace and without resistance (Tozzer 1941, note 271).

When the Spaniards were gone, famine brought the Maya to a low point, and when the Spaniards returned in 1541 they no longer recognized the country (Tozzer 1941, p. 55). The rain bringers, the *Chacob* Rain Gods, and *Itzam Na* and his consort, *Ix Chebel Yax,* were powerless to control the harvests.

In the 1540s, the Spanish *entrada* into Yucatan began for the third time (see Chamberlain 1966, pp. 202–236). Moving first into the camp at Champoton, the Montejos (the Elder, the Younger, and the Nephew) found the settlement in chaos. The Spaniards were close to starvation, the natives near rebellion, and supplies were low or nonexistent. Slowly gaining the support of native *caciques,* a settlement was secured at Campeche. Abandoning Champoton at the end of 1540, the Montejos and their entire army marched to Campeche. The final conquest of the Yucatan had begun.

In Campeche, Montejo the Younger summoned the *caciques* of a wide region, Ceh Pech, Ah Canul, Mani, and Ah Kin Chel, to appear before him and swear allegiance. Many of these western *caciques* obeyed his call. The Xiu of Mani quickly renewed their alliance with the Spanish forces to unite against the hated Cocom. Montejo the Younger began his slow move north, securing bases that were self-sufficient and part of a well-coordinated supply system. No group was isolated or in jeopardy of surprise attack. Each district was to be occupied and secured before the next move forward. Spanish rule was to be firmly organized, and good roads were laid out to guarantee secure conditions.

Late in 1541, Montejo the Younger led his entire force of 250 to 300 well-equipped Spanish soldiers and a large number of Indian warriors north to the Maya settlement of T-ho. On January 6, 1542, he founded Merida, the Spanish administrative capital of Yucatan.

From T-ho, Montejo the Younger planned to conquer Yucatan by peaceful means or war. He sent out a summons to the *caciques* of the region to report to him. Two or three caciques submitted, but most responded with fierce hostility. The Maya warriors approached the town, sent off arrows, and challenged the Spaniards to fight in the open. Montejo the Younger exerted every effort to win allegiance by peaceful means, but at the same time, he prepared his forces for war. The Maya resisted and set up strong fortifications at well-chosen points where they ambushed the Spanish soldiers. The Maya fled and hid in the bush, filled their wells with stones, destroyed their *milpas,* and destroyed their stores of corn.

Four months after the Spaniards had arrived at T-ho, the Maya attacked the encampment. Montejo the Younger immediately counterattacked with every one of his soldiers. The Maya ranks were broken, and the Spaniards fired into the Maya with small cannons, charged them with horses, trampled them, lanced them, and cut them down with swords. The dead Maya piled up and served as ramparts for the soldiers on horseback. The fighting fields were covered with bodies of the dead Indians. With this victory, the Spaniards secured the area around Merida, controlling the surrounding districts.

By the middle of 1542, Merida, like San Francisco de Campeche to the southwest, was firmly established. The entire west and north coasts of Yucatan and the western interior provinces, like Mani, were under Spanish control. The men of armor and the cross were now ready to turn to the east coast and to the southern provinces. Sotuta, Cochuah, the Cupul province, and Uaymil-Chetumal, the most powerful and most warlike of the Maya *cacicazgos,* still remained free and independent territories.

Montejo the Younger moved against Sotuta and against Nachi Cocom. The Cocom province was prepared to repel the entry of the Spaniards. When Montejo the Younger proclaimed that the Maya should submit to the Spanish crown and the Christian cross, the Cocom warriors refused. The Spanish attacked and were able to subjugate the province. Defeated on the battlefield, the proud Nachi Cocom was forced to accept the overlordship of the hated Spanish conquistadors; Nachi Cocom was also baptized and took the name Juan.

The nephew of Montejo the Father had been assigned to conquer the eastern Maya of the Chikinchel, Tazes, and Ecab provinces. Moving east, he established the town of Valladolid on May 24, 1543. He appointed the town's officials, designated some 40–50 soldiers as citizens, and assigned them land in and around the town. For the labor needed to construct public buildings, a church and dwellings, he drafted natives from the surrounding pueblos of Kanxoc, Tixhualatun, and others.

According to legend, when Valladolid was founded on the site of Saci, the powerful military and religious capital of Cupul, an enormous tree was growing in the center of town. This most unusual tree provided fruits of all kinds in its branches. One man, Caamal, was one of many men taken from Kanxoc to Saci by the Spanish troops as part of a labor draft. This man was assigned to work with other Maya to cut down the great tree. The men worked in shifts cutting and chopping at the enormous tree. When Caamal cut at the living tree, he saw it bleed. All day, the men chopped at the enormous tree that had stood in the center of Saci since ancient times. Its roots reached into the ancestors' Under-

world, and its branches grew into the realm of the Sky Gods. The men worked in shifts chopping down the tree until early evening. Then, the workers rested and slept through the night. When morning came, the men returned to work, and the tree had healed itself. Not a cut nor a wound on its trunk could be seen. The Spanish overlords were furious, and the men were set to work again. They chopped at the tree, the tree that gave all types of fruit, and they marveled at it, wondered at it, and feared it. The Spaniards made them cut at the tree all morning, all afternoon, and through the night. When the man who was called Caamal saw that the tree had healed itself and then saw the tree of his ancestor's time bleeding again, he moved away, and with his head down, walked league after league to his hut in Kanxoc. When he entered his home, the man who was called Caamal sat on his mat and wept.

The eastern Maya *caciques* had accepted Spanish rule only after bitter defeat, and they prepared themselves to resist time and time again. In 1532 and 1534, the Yucatec Maya had driven the Spaniards out of Ciudad Real de Chichen Itza and out of the Uaymil-Chetumal province in the southeast corner of the Maya realm. The proud and independent Maya believed that what they had once achieved would repeat itself again.

Having lost Saci as a capital, the Cupul moved to organize other pueblos whose *caciques,* war leaders, and priests had secretly contacted neighboring *principales* to organize perhaps the greatest coalition Yucatan had ever known (see Chamberlain 1966; pp. 237–252; Bricker 1981, pp. 18–19). The *Chilam Balam* excited the Indian populations to a high, frenzied enthusiasm to exterminate the Spaniards and drive them from the Maya land. The plans for the rebellion were secret, and the Spaniards, unknowing, believed the Maya were finally conquered. On the night of November 8, 1546, or the dates 5 *Cimi* 19 *Xul* in the Maya calendar, the eastern Maya made a united effort to throw off Spanish domination. The date in the Maya calendar translated "death" and "the end," signified the end of Spanish domination and death to all the foreign intruders.

With the rising full moon, the Maya rose in rebellion and fury. The greatest concentration of force was in the Cupul province, focused in and around Valladolid. Any Spaniards who were in the pueblos around the city were slaughtered. Spaniards were crucified by the Maya and left out under the tropical sun to burn or be pierced by arrows. Other Spaniards were captured, tortured, and sacrificed. Two Spanish children were roasted over *copal* (incense), and others were sacrificed by Maya priests, their chests cut open, and their hearts torn out (Chamberlain 1966, p. 241). When the Indians reached the homes of the *encomenderos* (Spanish landowners), they killed them and slaughtered all the animals brought by the foreigners, horses, cattle, chickens, cats, and dogs. The trees and plants that the Spaniards had brought with them from Europe were uprooted. Every last trace of their presence was destroyed (Chamberlain 1966, p. 241).

On November 15, 1546, the Spaniard, Tamayo Pacheco, marched rapidly out of Merida with 40 Spaniards and 500 Indians to aid the besieged Valladolid. The Spanish forces moved through hostile territory where the Maya blockaded roads and barricaded their pueblos. Fighting hard the entire way, the troops broke through and entered Valladolid in 14 days. Tamayo Pacheco assumed command of the city on November 22, and with 60 Spanish soldiers and the support of Indians, they broke the blockade of the city. Pacheco moved his forces out of the city to reconquer the area of rebellion. The Maya, in turn, fortified their towns, deserted their pueblos when they could not defend them, destroyed their food supplies, and ambushed the Spanish forces at every opportunity.

By March 1547, the Spanish troops had subdued the great revolt in all but the peripheral zones. The *cacicazgos* of the Cupul and the Cocom, among other eastern provinces, were reconquered. When Spanish control was restored, the principal leaders of the revolt in various districts were identified, and five or six were executed or burned, including a Chilam Balam, who claimed to be the Son of God. The power to punish was wielded with greater harshness than ever before by the Father and Younger Montejos, who were almost invariably moderate (Chamberlain 1966, p. 250). For example, Montejo the Nephew captured 25 Cupul with weapons in their hands; their hands were chopped off without mercy. During the revolt, the Spaniards and their allies of Champoton and Campeche enslaved about 2000 enemy Indians, including women and children, a great many of whom were Cupul (Chamberlain 1966, p. 250). The Great Revolt had reduced the eastern and southern provinces to chaos and poverty. Pueblos lay deserted, and Indians left their homes permanently, some migrating as far south as the distant and still free Petan Itza.

To restore order, Montejo the Elder called the native *caciques* to assemble in Merida. Here, he told them that it was his purpose to govern with justice and equality for the benefit of the province and all its people. He promised that any Spaniard who harmed an Indian would be punished and that the Maya lords should release all prisoners that had been taken as slaves. "Why," he asked, "why did you rise up in rebellion." The Maya Lords replied, "Not because of the ill-treatment from the *castellanos*. It was the native priests, the *Chilam Balam* who were responsible for the war, the revolution, and the rebellion."

The Mayan Lords, downcast, returned in shame to their pueblos. One Chilam Balam *looked at his 13-year-old daughter brutally raped by a Spanish soldier. Another Maya Lord looked at his pueblo that was abandoned and burned by Spanish soldiers. One Lord looked for his wife killed by the Spanish army. Another Lord sat in shock, bemoaning the loss of his young son and beautiful daughter; he would never know whether they were captured by the army, dead or alive, servant or free. Slowly, the craftsmen returned to work and the* milpero *began to cut the forest. The House of Armor and the Cross had subdued the Maya, but the flames of rebellion would burn again and again.*

The Yucatec Maya resisted political domination by the Spaniards longer than any other native group in Mesoamerica (see Bricker 1981). By 1547, although the Spaniards declared victory, the eastern Maya and those who fled south to the Peten area remained independent for another 150 years. Much more difficult than the political domination of the Maya were the battles fought for their souls (see Chamberlain 1966, pp. 311–329; Bricker 1981, pp. 20–21).

In 1549, seven friars entered Yucatan with Nicolas de Albalate, who was returning to Yucatan after completing a mission in Spain. Among the seven newcomers was the young friar, Diego de Landa, who would become regional head of the Franciscans and, eventually, Bishop of Yucatan. The Franciscan order grew in the Yucatan, having obtained permission from the Spanish crown for the exclusive right of the *doctrina,* Christianization of the Indians, to the exclusion of any other order of regular clergy. As part of their "mission," the Franciscans established themselves as advocates of the Indians, defending them from abuses and promoting their welfare (Chamberlain 1966, p. 318). They opposed Indian slavery, excessive tribute, and excessive services under the *encomienda* system. Their recommendations and charges could be considered exclusively political in character, often being concerned with governance rather than salvation. The Franciscans divided the Yucatan into districts and established monasteries or convents in Campeche, Mani, Merida, and Izamal. They established schools and provided religious instruction to native children and adults. The Indians provided the religious order with support, paid tribute to the clergy, and supplied the labor force to build the massive stone religious structures. But Maya culture was too ancient, sophisticated, and advanced to be swept to the side by the invading friars (Chamberlain 1966). It could be modified, but it could not be destroyed.

Elements of the Maya religion defied eradication as native ritual, idolatry, and even human sacrifice continued (see Bricker 1981, p. 20). In 1562, Father Diego de Landa initiated the Inquisition in the Yucatan. The accusations of idolatry, falling from the true faith, began in Mani in the western province and continued to Sotuta in the eastern area. These were unlucky times under the Maya calender (Bricker 1981, p. 20), and 156 Maya leaders were imprisoned in Merida. These men were severely tortured, hot wax was dripped on their naked bodies, they were hung by ropes from the waist, whipped, tied to the *burro* (the wooden frame), tortured, permanently maimed, or killed. The Maya were brutalized in this way to confess to transgressions and be saved.

Two centuries later in 1761, Jacinto Canek sat shivering in a Merida jail (see Bricker 1981). He wore a white cotton tunic and trousers, the uniform of the Maya campesino (farmer). The covering did no good, with him sitting on the cold, damp stone floor. Canek was from the small town of Quisteil, just 6 leagues from Sotuta, ancient capital of the mighty Cocom. He was drunk the night when he cried out against the Spaniards. Weeping, he told his friends to throw off the yoke of servitude and fight the Spaniards to the end. And now, here he sat in the jail, which was cold as a tomb. Canek heard the guards approach-

ing his cell. *The boots of the guards were unmistakable, loudly they pounded down the path to his cell, heavily crushing what was lying under their bootheels. The uniformed men unlocked the door, and marching in, they saw a small man draped in a pure white cotton manta huddled against the wall. The last king of the fierce Itza had the same name as this so-called instigator of the revolt at Quisteil,* Kan ek'. *He was the* lucero, *the morning star. The guards pulled Canek to his feet. They marched him down the corridor into a chamber where they tortured him, broke his arms, and crushed his legs. They tore the flesh off his body with pinchers and finally smashed his skull, ending his misery. His body was burned and the ashes thrown into the sky to be carried by the wind—ashes of the rebellion cast over the land. Eight other Indian leaders were hung, their bodies quartered and publically displayed. Other Indian prisoners were whipped, and their right ears were chopped off. In July of 1762, the Indian town of Quisteil was leveled—all traces of the town obliterated. The rebellion was in ruins, the flames quelled, but in the wind the ashes carried the spirit of Canek and deposited it over the land.*

From 1762 to 1812, half a century, the Maya slept beneath the blanket of Spanish control. The *encomendero* (entrusted ones) replaced the defeated (and often dead) Indian Lords by continuing to collect tribute and command the services that, before the conquest and colonial administration, had gone to the Indian rulers (Simpson 1937:9).

THE HOUSE OF *HENEQUEN,* HOUSE OF SUGARCANE, AND HOUSE OF *YUM CIMIL* (THE LORD OF DEATH) (A.D. 1812–1915)

After the Mexican War of Independence (1810–1812), the Spanish crown no longer controlled Indian labor. A new class of rulers, creoles, those born in New Spain of strict Spanish descent, stepped in to control the Indians. After independence, poverty persisted, with large numbers of *campesinos* scratching out a meager living. Many Indians became landless and were no longer protected by the Spanish crown. The Indians lived under the tropical sun and petitioned for rain from the *Chac* Rain Gods. The climate was dry, the crops failed, frustration grew, and the flames of fury rose up to explode into the bloody Caste War of Yucatan (Figure 5.3) (see Reed 1964; Montes de Oca 1977; Bricker 1981; Muñoz 1981).

Francisco May stared at his brother Teodosio May, covered with blood. "There is no food to the south," Teodosio told Francisco. "No food for us. All the best land has been taken by the sugar plantation patrones. *Foreigners have taken our land, brother, from the first instant they entered our territory—the Spanish foreigners, the Mexicans, the blancos—they all came to take the land." Francisco May was aware that new laws had been created in Mexico permitting communal land to be taken from the pueblos. Some towns transferred land to a trusted elder, and he held the title or the town's communal property. Without this protection, the pueblos were being stripped of their land. How could they*

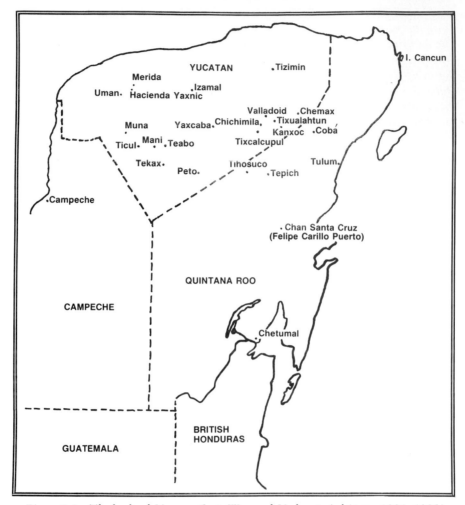

Figure 5.3. The lowland Maya—Caste War and Modern period (A.D. *1821–1985*).

survive with no land? *Many of the young men in the village moved onto the sugarcane or henequen plantations* (Figure 5.4). *Many were treated in the same manner as his younger brother, Bonifacio. The young men became deeper and deeper in debt to the hacienda store. They were no more than slaves; it was a time of slavery. They were treated like dogs. He remembered his younger brother when he returned home. He was starved, beaten, bruised, half dead, crushed beneath the boot of the henequen plantation overseer and his assistant. Francisco closed his eyes and crushed his fists on his temples. What was to happen in this evil time?*

In the center of Kanxoc, in front of the holy church, a Mayan campesino stood in front of the crowd. "They have asked the dzulob *priests to come and make us stop fighting. Jacinto Pat, Cecilio Chi, Bonifacio Novelo, Jose Maria Cocom, and Venancio Pec have sent a letter asking what the* dzulob *priests did*

Figure 5.4. Henequen *field in northwestern Yucatan.*

when Father Herrera abused the poor Indians. Herrera put a horse's saddle on a poor Indian, mounted him, whipped him, and opened his belly with his spurs. Where were the dzulob priests when this happened?" The campesino asked, "Where were the priests when the chief of Peto arrested Manuel Antonio Ay? Where were they when he was taken to Valladolid and executed?" The Indian *spoke again, "Where were the* dzulob *priests when Trujeque's troops entered Tepich looking for Cecilio Chi? Where were they when the troops murdered our families, looted our homes, and burned down our houses? Where were the priests when the* dzul *officer raped the young Indian girl? Trujeque brought five Indian prisoners into Tihosuco and shot them to death. Where were the priests?" Francisco May listened to these words and understood why his brother Teodosio followed Cecilio Chi in murdering the rich* dzulob *families of Tepich (see Bricker 1981).*

The struggle between foreigner and Maya surfaced again. The blancos saw rebellion in the eyes of their servants, became hysterical, and the witch hunt began. Francisco Uc, despite being the *cacique* of Uman and a wealthy, educated gentleman, was still an Indian. He was arrested and condemned with other dark-skinned native *caciques,* was stood before a firing squad, and was murdered. After the execution of Manuel Antonio Ay and *caciques* like Francisco Uc, the distinction between castes was clear. The blancos and the Maya began a war that would last more than 50 years.

Jacinto Pat and Cecilio Chi led the rebellion of the eastern Maya. The time had come to change the ruling class of Yucatan. The seat of power was to be filled by the Maya. In Merida while the blancos fought among themselves, they allowed the Maya to gain control of Tixcacalcupul and Tihosuco. Also, the Maya gained control over Valladolid and moved west to Peto. In April of 1848, negotiations were made to end the war. Jacinto Pat was appointed governor of all the Indians of Yucatan, a position equal to the white governor. The eastern Maya under Cecilio Chi were not willing to accept Pat as governor; in fact, they were not willing to accept anyone. Chi's lieutenant, Raimundo Chi, marched to Peto with 1500 men, caught Pat by surprise, demanded and received the staff, banner, and treaty and destroyed them on the spot. Meanwhile, Cecilio Chi attacked Teabo and Mani killing more than 200 people. The treaty was over, and the war raged on. In May of 1848, Ticul was abandoned by the blancos and fell into Maya hands. The Maya gathered on the outskirts of Campeche and a few kilometers outside of Merida. Camped there for the final assault on Merida in 1848 the Maya leaders prepared for the attack, but the Maya soldier came and said, "Xickanic" ("I am going"). He and others like him packed up their goods and slipped out of camp. June and July were planting times, so the Maya retreated to tend their fields. Fiercely independent, they had pushed the ladinos back, gave themselves room, wanted no one to rule over them, and disappeared into the forest to tend to their fields and their families.

During the remaining months of 1848, the *blancos* pushed back. They moved east to Yaxcoba, Valladolid, Tekax, Tihosuco, and marched into Maya towns. Defeat brought conflict, and in 1849, Jacinto Pat and Cecilio Chi were murdered within months of each other (Bricker 1981, p. 102). Jacinto Pat was murdered by Venancio Pec who was one of his own soldiers, and Chi was murdered by his mestizo secretary who had been sleeping with Chi's wife. After this murder, Chi's compatriots mutilated his unfaithful wife and hacked her lover to death.

Francisco May and his brother, Bonifacio May, attended Cecilio Chi's funeral. The soldiers washed his body, dressed him in pure white clothing, and buried him. He was the most dreaded rebel, a spiritual descendant of Canek, Kan ek', or the morning star, that lighted the way and created a path for the Maya to follow, which was a path that led to rebellion, destruction, and the recreation of structure and power.

Kanxoc was a village that stood on the border with Valladolid located to the north and controlled by the blancos and Chan Santa Cruz located to the south and controlled by the fierce Cruzob, who were followers of the *Tatich* ("Patron of the Talking Cross") and the *Tata Naz* ("Speaker for the Talking Cross").

Francisco May sat in his hut twining henequen. His wife squatted before the fire, patting the masa (corn dough), making the tortillas. Outside, Bonifacio tended his bees with Francisco's son, Silvestre. Francisco's older brother, Teodosio, had recently returned from the southern Cruzob settlement of Santa Cruz de Bravo.

The Cruzob, *tatichos,* had gathered at Santa Cruz. When a blanco was seen by them, they killed him with their arrows. They were fierce men who wore one gold earring, and rather than wearing clothes made of cotton, they wore tunics and pants made of coarse plant fiber. The settlement of Santa Cruz was protected by traps dug along the trails leading into the town. Sharpened poles were placed in holes, and these traps were lightly covered. Twice the *federales* (Mexican police) came to Santa Cruz, and both times they were slaughtered. The Cruzob collected arms from the slaughtered men and also bought arms from the English of Belize to the south. Santa Cruz de Bravo was a fortified town.

Francisco May, his brothers, Bonifacio, and Teodosio, and his son, Silvestre, were involved in this struggle for power between the blancos and the Maya.
There was a man in Kanxoc, a rich man, who owned a hacienda. He completely closed off his land. Francisco and his brothers needed land to plant corn and grow crops to feed their families. There was no land for the members of the village to farm. Francisco May told his brothers, "We must farm the hacienda land. We can take a piece of the hacienda. We can take a very small piece to farm, to grow food to feed our families." Francisco, Bonifacio, and Teodosio moved onto the hacienda land to farm. They took a very small piece of land to farm. Their neighbors, desperate for land, also took very small pieces of land to make milpa. The hacendado (hacienda owner) went to Valladolid to complain to the authorities. He told them, "The Indians are on my land. They have moved onto the hacienda, and you must remove them. Get them off my land." The president of Valladolid sent a commission to Kanxoc. The commission entered the town, and the people of Kanxoc gathered in front of the church. "You must leave the hacienda land," the men from Valladolid told the men of Kanxoc. "It is not your land. You must not make milpa on hacienda land. It is prohibited." Tomas May came from Santa Cruz de Bravo to Kanxoc. He brought rifles with him and spoke to the men of Kanxoc. "Get guns," he told them. "Collect 150

rifles." The federales marched from Valladolid to Kanxoc to tell the people to leave the hacienda lands. More troops would come to remove the Indians if they didn't leave the hacienda lands. When the federales were marching out of Kanxoc, Tomas May shot the last soldier in the back. "The federales will return," Tomas May warned the men of Kanxoc. "You must prepare yourselves. Build a defensive rampart to protect yourselves." The women and children of the town fled into the monte (forest). They fled to small casitas (huts) in their milpas. Only the men remained in the town. Fifty federales marched into the town of Kanxoc, but the village was abandoned. The men of Kanxoc positioned themselves between Valladolid and Kanxoc, protected by the earth ramparts. The federales climbed to the church tower, and the men of Kanxoc fired on them (Figure 5.5). The town was surrounded, and the federales were trapped in the center. The federales and the men of Kanxoc signaled to one another with the bugle. The federales signaled for peace, and Tomas May signaled "No." At dusk, the bugle signaled "Oracion" (the end of the day). Night passed, and at dawn, the bugle signaled "La Diana." The day and the next night passed.

In Valladolid, the president of the town wondered what had happened to the 50 federales who had marched to Kanxoc. He sent 100 more federales to Kanxoc. These 100 men were entering the territory of Kanxoc when they heard from the center of town the bugle signaling "Peace." From the surrounding ramparts, they heard "Degüello" (attack without mercy). The 100 federales, believing their companions were charging the town, charged. Federales in the church fired desperately on the federales charging from the outskirts of the town, and in less than 20 minutes, many of the "enemy" were dead or dying. From the ramparts, the men of Kanxoc advanced, marched into the town, and stood in front of the holy church. There, they killed all of the federales who were still alive. They cut off their heads and ate their brains. Francisco May saw the dead men; blood was everywhere. His brother Teodosio smashed the head of a dying federale thinking of the brutal murder of his friend, Manuel Antonio Ay. Bonifacio and Francisco's son, Silvestre, walked among the dead and dying federales, and Bonifacio thought of the beatings he had received from the hacendado's overseer. Silvestre May led his uncle away from the plaza to his home. Francisco May picked up rifles, one for himself, another for his brother Teodosio, and a third for his son Silvestre. "It is time," he thought, "time to move south. I will take my family, and we will disappear into the monte. We will travel south to Santa Cruz. Tomas will guide us, and we will live deep in the forest, my brothers, my son, and I. Someday, my son may return to Kanxoc, but the federales will be back soon and we must be gone."

The federales did return but with a white flag petitioning for peace. The Kanxoc people had guns and were prepared to repel them—prepared to fight all the time. A horse-drawn cart entered the town. Men loaded the dead federales on the cart and drove it back to Valladolid. The hacendado left Kanxoc; he went to Valladolid where, according to oral history, he was killed by the president of Valladolid because of all the problems he had caused.

During this time the Maya lived in the *monte*. Whole families lived in the *monte* cutting the bush, firing it, and making *milpa*. The Cruzob maintained

Figure 5.5. The church tower on the plaza in the village of Kanxoc.

control over the settlement of Santa Cruz de Bravo until 1901 when the Mexican general, Ignacio Bravo, occupied it. A few months later, the President of Mexico, Porfirio Dias, set in motion a plan to create a federal territory. Quintana Roo was established in November of 1902. In 1915, the federal troops abandoned Chan Santa Cruz, and the Cruzob, having regained their settlement, destroyed the railroad—burned the train coach cars, tore the engines apart, and tore up the tracks. The telephone and telegraph lines were cut. Not long after this, a smallpox epidemic hit, and most of the Cruzob leaders died. After the epidemic, the Cruzob split into two groups. The northern group with headquarters at Chunpom was led by Juan Bautista Vega. The southern group, with headquarters at Yokdzonot Guardia, was led by General Francisco May. Later, General May lived in Chan Santa Cruz until his death in 1969 (see Reed 1966).

THE HOUSE OF THE CHACOB (THE RAIN GODS) (A.D. 1930–1987)

The whole society remained divided into western and eastern sections. To the west, where the henequen grew, haciendas held control. Resources were bundled for export and status positions ranked either very high or very low, governor or servant, ruler or slave. But to the east, where the sun rose, the Maya grew corn, the elders ruled in villages, and a father controlled his family on *ranchos* located deep in the forest. Resources were used for subsistence, and status positions were given and taken away. The eastern territory of Quintana Roo was a frontier beyond tight control of state government. In the eastern sector in small villages and on native *ranchos,* the elders organized labor. Political leaders cajoled members of the community to clear paths and plazas, and traditional priests, the *h-menob,* managed rituals and carried out ceremonies to gods that were thousands of years old. The political system was loose, non-hierarchical, and minimally bureaucratic. The *delegado* (mayor) of the village and the *presidente* of the *ejido* (see Simpson 1937) negotiated or mediated and then returned to their normal activities of hunting, farming, tending bees, or planting fruit trees. Contact with the *federales* was minimal and avoided. When the Maya saw the police on the roads, they disappeared into the rainforest.

Don Silvestre May was living in Kanxoc with his brothers. The high rainforest around the town had been cut, and harvests were beginning to fail. He met with his brothers and said, "I have heard of land to the east, a small settlement of chicleros. It is a land of high rainforest, rich black soil, good hunting, and clear water. We should go and cut chicle, hunt, and, perhaps, cut milpa." The brothers agreed, and the three men traveled east, 12 leagues, a two-day walk. When they reached Coba, Lencho was living there. He was the only one living along the lakes. Lencho had his rancho and a corral of cattle. When Don Silvestre saw Coba, he decided to settle there. The first time he came to Coba was with his brothers, and they built a lean-to with a thatch roof to protect them from the rain. The crude and temporary structure had no sides. They hung hammocks from the rafters and at night heard the frogs sing. In the early morning, the birds would begin to call. Through the night, the sounds changed, and Don Silvestre would sleep and then wake up in blackness and know where he was in the passage of the night. The darkness would fade, and in morning light, he would see the hammocks of his brothers. Under the thatched roof surrounded by the forest,

*they had no leader. The three brothers worked as one body. They made choco-
late over the fire and drank it out of half gourds. Squatting around the fire, they
ate day-old tortillas with some chile. Then the brothers would march off to cut
zapote to collect chicle and, later, cut the forest down to prepare their milpas.
Next they would hunt in the forest for deer, jabali (wild pig), or wild turkey. They
were equals, alone in the forest, free to take land and use it, free to use resources they found, and free to make decisions. The three brothers planted their
fields and walked along trails through the forest back to Kanxoc. They waited for
the months to pass and periodically checked their fields. When they saw that the
harvest was ready, they moved their families to Coba.*

Don Silvestre came with his son, Jose Asuncion, and his two sons-in-law,
Panfilo Canche and Pedro Celestino Noh, to settle in Coba. Jose Maria Caamal came from Kanxoc, a *compadre* of Don Silvestre's. The people from
Kanxoc settled on the south side of Lake Coba. To the north of the lake,
people came from the town of Tixhualatun. Don Fernando Cen and Bernabel
Cen came with other families from Tixhualatun. When these families came
to Lake Coba, there was no village, no *ejido*. It was national forest, pure
rainforest. The governance of the settlement lay in the hands of the older
members of the families. The settlement formed a village, and the first *delegado* was Don Fernando Cen. The *delegado* was "the father of all" and was
supposed to be above reproach, to be just, and to keep the village calm and
tranquil. He was the justice. If a pig went into a *milpa,* the *milpero* went to
the *delegado,* and the *delegado* then went to see the owner of the pig. The
value of the ruined *elote* (corn) was stated, and the offender had to pay the
fine. If someone was drunk, the *delegado* threw him in jail for the night. If
the guilty party wouldn't pay the fine, then the *delegado,* the offender, and
the plaintiff went to Cozumel, where the offender had to pay double and he
had to pay for the trip.

Don Fernando Cen was the first *delegado* of Coba (Figure 5.6). He
watched over the townsfolk and treated them as though they were his family. He worked in his small store, providing goods that people needed,
including sugar, coffee, candles, matches, and sometimes corn. He lent
money when people had an emergency, but mainly, he opened his doors and
provided a place to sit and gossip, to share thoughts and news, and to rest for
a moment. People came to complain, redress offenses, and set their lives on
a normal course again. He made sure that people had access to water from
the wells in the town plaza or from the cenotes. He held festivals now and
then to collect and redistribute foodstuffs. He acted as the mediator between
the village and the larger society.

Years passed, and the village grew as more families moved to Coba. Jose
Isabel Cocom was elected *delegado*. He had heard that a school was to be
built in Coba, so he came to live in the village. He helped build the school in
1971, and his grandchildren entered the very first classes. He built a house
for himself and a house for his children and grandchildren. He built a cook-
house and an outside oven to bake bread. He planted trees and kitchen gar-

Figure 5.6. Don Fernando Cen, the first delegado *(mayor) of Coba.*

dens in his yard area and cut, burned, and planted his *milpa,* and harvested
his crops. He lived in Coba with his wife, his children, and his grandchildren.
For three years he held the office of *delegado.* He was a respected elder and
worked with the other men in the village to create the *ejido* of Coba. The el-

ders prepared papers to submit, and the men of Coba cut a trail to demarcate the proposed lines of the *ejido*. In 1972, 38 men signed the papers for the creation of the *ejido* of Coba, and 3800 hectares of land were granted and demarcated in the national forest.

The next *delegado* was elected. One night, while he was drinking, he got into a fight. Afterwards, the people of Coba did not want him to be *delegado* any longer. His family would not pay for his damages, and plantiffs were not paid for damages even though the offenders had paid him. The mayor was giving presents to the president of the *municipio,* so the president wanted him to stay in office, but the people of Coba voted him out.

The next *delegado* was an elder in the community, a master carpenter, and a master house builder. He entered the office in troubled times. He told the men of the village that on Sunday, they had *fagina* (communal labor for the welfare of the community). The men gathered on Sunday to clear the plaza area on the south side of the lake. The following Sunday, the plaza on the north side of the lake was to be cleared; however, people living on the south side of the lake refused to come to work. At the same time, the people of Coba were unhappy with the guardians of the Ruins of Coba. All of the guardians were men from the town of Chemax located far to the north of Coba. The government paid the guardians a large salary, more than 10 times the daily wage of a worker in Coba. The members of the Coba *ejido* told the guardians that if one more guardianship was assigned to a person from Chemax, all of the guardians would have to leave Coba. Also, the *ejido* members complained that the guardians were drinking all the time and not really doing any work. Also during this time, outsiders came to Coba to build a tourist hotel. The construction team came into Coba and began to clear the land. Daniel Cen, *presidente* of the Coba *ejido,* told the engineers that they must not continue the work. They were working on *ejido* land and had not obtained permission to do so. He was able to stop the work. Meanwhile, the mayor went to the *municipio* center on the island of Cozumel to report these problems. The governor sent a letter informing the mayor that he would visit Coba to see how it was with the people in the village. No one was told. The mayor was afraid the people of Coba would think of and report problems to the governor. One of two Cobaeños traveled to Tulum on the east coast and saw the announcement that the governor of the state was coming to visit Tulum and Coba. They spread this news in Coba, and when the governor arrived, the people of Coba were gathered at the school to meet with him. "We want a new mayor," they told the governor. Shortly afterward, Daniel Cen was elected the new *delegado*. On the following Sunday, he gave a fiesta to the town; he killed two pigs and brought in 50 kilograms of tortillas from Tulum. The people drank beer and soft drinks.

The next mayor was elected mayor primarily by the women of Coba. When he was elected to office, he was a Pentecostal Church member, and he did not drink. Soon afterward though, he stopped going to church; he started drinking heavily, and people said he no longer gave good justice.

Finally, Florentino Cen became the next *delegado* of Coba. The times had changed. In the time of Don Fernando Cen, the first *delegado,* the village was small and familylike. Political action was informal and nonbureaucratic, and there were no policemen living in Coba. The village was fairly isolated, and there was no paved road into the village. People walked to Kanxoc, Tixhualatun, and Chemax to visit family who had remained in these parent villages. By the time Don Esteban Cen became mayor, there was a paved road into town, the village had grown, and the two sectors of the village, the northside and the southside of the lake, had become discrete entities with very localized interests. Outsiders from Chemax were guardians of the ruins and making a fortune compared with what the *milperos* of Coba earned. This introduced conflict and tension into the village. A few years before Don Esteban Cen became mayor, one of the guardians had mysteriously drowned in the lake with his head badly smashed. The tension was also obvious in the aberrant behavior of Don Esteban Cen's wife, who deposited "cow pies" in Jeeps and burned thatch roofs that protected stone statues in the ruins. She ended up in the village jail and afterward left town with her young daughter, quietly and quickly, never to return. She later committed suicide, and Don Esteban remarried.

When Florentino Cen became mayor, the villagers of Coba were not at all isolated from the outside world. The village had a large hotel with a variety of tourists. The stores that had in the past catered to the needs of village farmers now catered to the tourist trade. Buses roared into town on a fairly regular schedule, restaurants were opened, and liquor licenses were issued. The mayor no longer was a full-time *milpero*. The relatively wealthy people in the village were clearly distinguishable from the poorer families in town. The population of the town was exploding. Coba was the recipient of an *aqua potable* (potable drinking water) system given by the governor of the newly formed state of Quintana Roo. Electric lines were merely 20 kilometers outside of town. The modern comforts were closing in on the Maya.

Throughout Maya history, the political situation has been a very complicated one. Through time, simple familial systems of governing expanded into complex, bureaucratic organizations of power. As the cycle of time spun around, these two extreme forms of government, two extreme forms of political order, ebbed and flowed. As the village of Coba entered the modern era and was pulled into the bureaucratic organization of the state of Quintana Roo, far away from the plazas, far from the center of the town, life continued as it has for thousands of years.

The old man sat stiffly on the stool and made plans with his son for the upcoming ceremonies (Figure 5.7). The son half listened and fiddled with the dials on an old radio. He was trying to tune in the news to hear who had won the baseball game between Coba and Marcario Gomez. The old man patiently told his young son what he would need. "I need candles and gourds, sticks to bend into arcs, some flowers, and a cross made of wood." The son nodded his head. "We will hold the Lolcatali *ceremony in front of the rancho," the old man told him. "It will protect us. We will petition the spirits, walk around the property nine*

Figure 5.7. Don Demetrio Pol at his rancho, Chac Ne.

times, drink 13 bowls of balche wine, and pray to the alux. The balam wind spirits will be called to protect us. We will prepare nohua, the ritual bread, and slaughter a chicken. We will walk to the four corners, and there we will position the crosses, the pieces of the tancazche wood, a little rum, and some pieces of the black obsidian to protect us. We will offer the nohua and the balche to the alux.'' *It was the oldest ceremony, that of a father protecting his family. The old man would recite the chants at the altar. The copal incense would burn. He had fasted for 20 days and had not lain with his wife. His wife had pierced her ear lobe, and he had gathered the corn kernels and thrown them to divine the future.*

At the very end of the ceremony, weak from fasting, intoxicated by the *balche* and the rum, his head full of the incense smoke, the old man was transformed for a moment. He had immense power that reached back to the time of his ancestors and forward, providing a vision of the future. He achieved power over space and resources, and he achieved a divine status as priest and ruler of his family living under the tropical canopy. Through his vision, his knowledge, and his lead, the history and future of the Maya were kept as a sacred trust. In this way, as an *h-men,* a traditional Maya priest, he was empowered.

6/The Supernatural World

Life begins warm and vital, and life ends cold and dark.

To explain this immense mystery, humans everywhere have created systems to bring order out of chaos. Some explanations have been quite simple, setting the supernatural realm in a system of binary opposites (Levi-Strauss 1962) such as sun and moon, culture and nature, raw and cooked, and male and female. This approach describes the supernatural world, begins analysis, and allows for interpretations of the human mind. A second approach provides a multifaceted description of the elements of the supernatural realm, a differential analysis of symbols, and an interpretation of human nature and destiny on many planes (Turner 1967). For the Maya, it is possible to reach back in time and see religious actions as social drama, with patterned sets of processes evolving through time. Rituals with music, dance and costume, and chants and trances become sacred narratives reflecting human adaptation to life under the tropical canopy.

THE SKY GODS (A.D. 600–900)

The young ruler of Coba was viewing his stone portrait where it stood in front of the round altar stone. In his hands of flesh, he held the staff of his office, and there before him, it was repeated—carved in stone (Thompson, Pollock and Charlot 1932, p. 135). *The staff sloped down to the west, and his bold head faced to the east. Here, the serpent-reptile* Itzam Na *set down in the western sky and was carried by the god-impersonator to rise up again in the east. The statue was a model of a cosmic journey. The crosses in the ruler's skirt were symbols of crossed sticks that were used by the living to plot the movement of the stars and planet Venus. Here, cosmic travel was portrayed, and the ruler, carved in stone, was an integral part of this celestial journey.*

Away from the temple in small, shaded rooms and in bright, sunny patios, the craftsmen were performing their tasks. From clay, they fashioned pottery. The cylindrical bowls and flared dishes were covered with scenes of the Underworld. These pots were made solely for internment with the rulers in their royal graves (Coe 1978; Robicsek and Hales 1981). *The craftsmen drew grotesque figures, including the Jaguar symbol of the night sun, roaming the Underworld—the personification of death itself. The mythical* Moan *bird was por-*

trayed, the emblem of death associated with bloodletting ceremonies. Dancing skeletons—and monkeys, deer, rabbits, dogs, foxes, toads, vultures, insects, and, as messengers to the Underworld, bats—appeared on the funerary pots. Sky bands were painted on them, and the characters of the Underworld. The potters worked together drawing symbols on pots to accompany the rulers in their final journey. The drawings told a mythic epic of how men would confront gods and, by wily acts, defeat them.

Nearby, another craftsman pounded the bark of the copo *tree* (Standley 1930, pp 245–246) *to make paper. Beside him sat his brother, who coated the pages with a thin lime solution. An elderly man watched his sons working as he painted the hieroglyphic text. He was concerned with making a record of time,* kin *(day, or sun) counts, 20-year cycles, or rotating and repeating* katun *cycles; he measured and recorded the movements of the sun, the moon, and the planets.*

Away from the core of the city, a group of craftsmen were working on a mural. Some of the murals recorded information about Musencab, *the Bee God,* Ek Chuah, *the Merchant God, and royal personages marching in a row. The murals were coded to reflect the Sky, the Earth and the Underworld, the three important sectors of the Maya universe.*

On the outskirts of town, a simple farmer stood talking to a local h-men. *The* milpero *was ready to burn his fields the next day and was asking the* h-men *to perform the* Tupp-kak *ceremony to make the ground cool again after the flames burned the brush. The elderly* h-men *agreed to hold the ceremony and cautioned the young farmer to seek the proper winds the next day. He also advised him to cut a fire break this year because the weather was extremely dry. The old man told him how much corn to plant. The old man inquired about the farmer's beehives, and told him that soon he would need to hold a ceremony to protect his hives and family. "And your* cacao *groves," the old man asked, "are they growing well in the damper soils of the cenote?" The young man replied that the changes that the old man had suggested had helped things work out much better. The old man nodded briefly and turned to walk away. He was ramrod straight as he walked along the path toward his home. His eyes sparkled as he looked this way and that, never missing one piece of information to use to protect his people. His religious actions were focused on the fields, the bees, and the orchards. His knowledge about the nature of these earthly things was great, and through ritual and recitation, he ensured that his people would survive.*

THE EARTH GODS (A.D. 900–1200)

It was bone dry at Chichen Itza, and the ruling elite were becoming frantic. Although the salt beds to the north were producing quantities to trade, people would starve without the corn harvest. It was the Rain Gods who were responsible, and the ruler made plans to petition the Chacob *to bring the clouds and rains to end the drought.*

In Coba, Kinchil Coba made arrangements to transport grains to the west. The peninsula was dry to the west, but in the east, it was more moist, and the

grain harvest had been good, providing not only enough to feed the local population but also to transport grain to the west. "The ancestors are caring for us,"
thought Kinchil Coba. He had been visiting Macanxoc, where the stone statues
of ancestors were worshipped. He had brought candles and pom, the sweet
smelling incense, to burn to speak to the ancestors—seeking their favor. The
prayers were chanted and repeated over and over again. "We are tied directly to
Itzam Na," Kinchil Coba thought. "He is the Creator and the Rain God."

Craftsmen in Coba were working on jade pendants and carving tiny jade
frogs. These offerings would be sent west to be used in the fire ceremony on the
rim of the Cenote Sagrado at Chichen Itza. Messengers would dive into the cenote and bring messages to the Lords of the Underworld.

At Chichen Itza, the craftsmen gathered up wooden idols painted blue, the
sacred color of the Rain God, and burned black by the addition of rubber and incense. Copper bells were collected, and pottery vessels, textiles, and objects of
flint, obsidian, coral, and pumice. These were carried on trays along the short
sacbe, or white road, to the mouth of the Cenote Sagrado as the drums and
turtleshell rattles kept up a frantic beat. As fires were burning around the cenote
rim, the lips around the mouth of the cenote seemed to drip with blood.

Seated around a small steambath were the high priests of the Kukulcan Cult,
or Cult of the Plumed Serpent (Figure 6.1). They sat on reed mats and, with
stingray spines, practiced autosacrifice, drawing blood from their arms,
tongues, and other fleshy parts of their body. In a trance state, they invited
priest-novices to their side and, with the end of the spine, mixed their blood with
that of the young men by pricking a quincunx on the cheeks of the young men.
These four dots in a square with another dot in the middle were a symbol of the
Maya world. Four gods held up the four corners of the earth, and in the center
grew a mighty ceiba tree, the Yaxche. The Chac Rain Gods resided in the four
corners, with one mighty Chac in the center. Four birds rested in the four corners, and from there, four winds blew. This was the sacred form of the world, reflected in the form of the pyramid-temple flattened onto a plane—four corners
and the center, or top, where the priest-transformer resided. With this initiation,
the novices began a priestly journey, absorbing knowledge as they were taught.
They learned about the Sky realm and the daily journey of Itzam Na across the
heavens. They were taught about the Earth realm and how the smallest plants
were markers for the coming of the old men, the Chacob, with rains to water the
crops. They were instructed concerning the bees, how to cure them of illnesses,
how to pray over them, and how to protect them from evil winds. The novices
were taught about forces in the Underworld, the old god who dwelt beneath the
earth in a dark, watery place where Waterlily-Jaguar swam between sunset and
sunrise.

The craftsmen attendants brought the bells, wooden idols, jade, and other
sacred offerings to the young men. The priest-novices wrists were tied behind
their backs, and messages to encourage the gods to send rain were whispered in
their ears. The senior priest walked with them along the sacbe to the rim of the
cenote and they were pushed into the gaping mouth of the Underworld and
devoured.

Figure 6.1. The Temple of Kukulcan at Chichen Itza.

Far from the Cenote Sagrado, *a farmer and his wife surveyed the night sky. They prayed to Mistress Moon, and in her fullness, they planted the seeds of the chile and the papaya. With the full moon, the crops would grow plump. The farmer was a sky watcher. He looked for the rain clouds and observed the moon. The* Chacob *were important enough for him to hold a ritual to propitiate them. The moon goddess* Ix Chel Yax *was revered by the woman as the goddess of pro-creation (Thompson 1970, p. 244). Under the full moon, the man and the woman created life.*

THE UNDERWORLD (A.D. 1283–1441)

The Itza rulers of Chichen Itza had escaped to the east and were traveling south as the prophets had advised after their divinations. At Mayapan, the ruler's son entered his household and, in the interior courtyard, made his way to the ancestral shrine. With mathematical precision, he practiced the esoteric art of numerology. He counted the days, added up the four patron dieties of the year, recited the names of the 13 carrier gods who supported time, 13 accompa-nying volitives, 4 year signs, 13-day numbers, the 20-day signs, and 260- and 365-year cycles. From the manipulation of the numbers, the young nobleman predicted the future. He threw down the five corn kernals, read his fortune, and shivered in fear. The future looked glum as the katun *cycle was ending and the fall of Mayapan was near. He looked at the idols in the* oratorio *(small house-hold shrine) and prayed softly to the revered ancestors. Nachi Cocom gathered his bundles and walked out the door. In front of the house, the porters stood up as he came out, ready to manage their loads, and travel south to trade.*

By the light of the full moon, the line of men snaked through the forest. They walked all night as the Waterlily-Jaguar struggled through the Underworld to rise up as the morning sun. At dawn, Nachi Cocom halted his line and, calling the men to stand around him, squatted down and recited a prayer to Ek Chuah, *the patron god of merchants. His assistant burned the* pom *incense in a censer and, with black soot taken from the fire, covered the body of Nachi Cocom. He covered the lips of Nachi Cocom with red paste. With a pack on his back and his spear-staff in his hand, Nachi Cocom danced to meet the morning sun. As the sun rose, its first rays struck the branches of the* cacao *trees and illuminated the god-impersonator of* Ek Chuah, *Nachi Cocom. After the prayers and the ritual, the men gathered* cacao *beans to trade in the south and added these to the packs.*

In Mayapan, the craftsmen were making idols. They made small carved fig-ures out of limestone to be set near altars or in shrines. Both old men with promi-nent noses and no teeth, symbolizing Itzam Na, and the handsome young Corn God were carved. Other craftsmen carved turtles that would be placed together near altars. Perhaps the great earth disk was represented here as the back of a turtle or a totem referring to a family. One young craftsmen gouged out the tur-tles back and fitted the hole with a stone lid. Inside the turtle container, he placed two tok *(obsidian flake blades used in bloodletting).*

In another court, craftsmen working with clay were making censers for burning offerings of pom *incense. The young man worked on building the censer, thinking of the offering he would make to the ancient* Chacob. *He pulled the clay, and the long nose appeared, and he curled it at the end. The diety was modeled toothless, and a scroll appeared beneath the eye. In the censer, the high priest would burn* pom, *and the black smoke would call the black thunderclouds.*

Beyond the city wall at Mayapan, a farmer made plans to hunt. As the sun disappeared beneath the horizon, he set up candles and prayed to the Sip, *the spirit protector of the deer in the forest. He lit a few candles and visualized the guardian spirit, a very tiny deer with enormous antlers and with a nest of wasps between them.*

With this vision in his mind, he blew out the candles and disappeared to hunt in the forest.

PROGNOSTICATION AND MAGIC (A.D. 1441–1511)

Mayapan had fallen, and the regional states vied for command over the peninsula. During this turbulent time, the *Chilam Balam* (Jaguar Speakers) voiced their prophecies. Time itself twisted and turned like the coils of a serpent and, turning around, repeated itself. The readers of the future were men learned about the past. As the cycle of time spun around, *katuns* of the same name would return with the same events. Not only was history believed to repeat itself but these repetitions were believed to occur in precise *katun* cycles that could be foretold by the prophets; and this led the Maya to keep time and manipulate it.

The baby was born on the fourth day of the month of Uo, *and they named him Balam (Jaguar), after their lineage. The fourth day was* Kan, *the corn sign, and the month* Uo *was the month of the frogs. For members of the Balam lineage, it was auspicious. He would be the rain bringer in the time of the frogs. He would be the prophet sent to make the corn grow.*

His parents watched over him and taught him the right path. He was quick to learn and remember, and the elders were pleased with him. As a child, he was often seated at the knee of his grandfather as the old man prepared plants to cure illness or recited prayers to chase the evil spirits away from the house or out of the village. He walked the paths to his grandfather's milpa, *and the old man reminded him of the medicinal plants found along the trail and how to prepare and use them. In the early morning, the old man would tell the boy stories about the* balam *spirits who guarded the four corners of the town and about the* alux *who were dwarf-tricksters but who would guard the fields if offerings were made. The ancient one told the boy how to call the* Chacob, *what prayers needed to be said, and how the altar was to be prepared. He taught the boy how to protect himself from evil winds like* tancazik *and which herbs to place above the doorway to guard the house. The child became a record of all that was good.*

The old h-men *knew that the boy was powerful with this knowledge, and the time came to send the boy away. When the boy became a young man and his grandfather was failing, the family sent him to town. He walked out of the forest into the town, where he entered the temple to prepare himself as a priest. The young man Balam, or "Jaguar–Night Sun," became* Ah Kin, *"He of the Sun." No longer did he dream of the* alux, *the* tun, *the old men who guarded the* milpa, *the* balam, *or the* sip. *Now, he was taught about the highest of deities,* Itzam Na *("Iguana House") and his consort,* Ix Chebel Yax. *The old agricultural deities were cast aside, and the God of Merchants* (Ek Chuah), *the Sun God* (Kinich Ahau), *and the Venus Cult* (Xix Ek *or "Wasp Star") became the important parts of his vision.*

As a priest, Ah Kin became learned. He was an astronomer, a mathematician, and a curer in addition to performing other priestly duties. Yet, he never forsook the teachings of his old grandfather, and his ties to the farmers were stronger than those of most other priests. One day he was relaxing in his quarters when the messenger came to tell him that his old grandfather had died. Ah Kin felt his eyes burning with tears, and closing his eyes, he looked deeply into the past, recounting the long life of his grandfather. Of all the stories that the old man had told him, the most vivid was the legend of the invasion of the peninsula by the Putun and Itza traders. As time turned its cycle, the prophet Ah Kin saw into the future. As a Chilam Balam, *Jaguar Speaker, he saw into the future and saw another invasion of the peninsula. The visions pained him because he could sense the violent penetration into and destruction of the old ways.*

RELIGIOUS SYNCRETISM (A.D. 1511–1812)

The Spaniards entered the peninsula for the first time from the east but were driven back into the sea. They entered the peninsula for the second time from the west and again failed. Finally, the last assault was made slowly and deliberately, like a turtle, and the invasion shook the Maya world to its very core.

Nachi Cocom and the people of his province, Sotuta, had been overrun by the Spaniards, and the invaders baptized the powerful ruler, Juan. As time passed, Nachi Cocom fell dreadfully ill, and his brother Lorenzo offered human sacrifices to save the ruler's life. After two months, Nachi Cocom still lay dying. Two boys were brought to the Christian church, and their hearts were offered to save the life of the *batab* (governor). Nachi Cocom died two days later and was buried in the church at Sotuta. His brother, Lorenzo, became *batab* and rebelled against the new religion and continued to practice the traditional rites of the Maya. In 1562, he had three boys taken to Chichen Itza, where they were thrown into the *Cenote Sagrado*. Later, in July of 1562, out of desperation and anticipation of Friar Diego de Landa's Inquisition, Lorenzo Cocom hanged himself.

It was not merely the religious contact that produced such a high degree of anxiety. It was the clash between cultures, shattering a cultural pattern that had shown brightly for a thousand years. It was the demographic crisis, the droughts, the famine, and the disease, unbalancing men, women, and children. It was the disruption of economic life and constant political struggles, setting noble against noble and ruler against ruled.

In Yucatan, it was not only the soldier that tramped into the Maya world but a new ideological framework carried in by Franciscan friars. The old religious hierarchy of Ah Kin and other high priests was crushed when Christian monasteries were built in the major centers of Spanish control. The Spaniards issued labor drafts and ordered the Maya to dismantle their temples to build sturdy churches. Although the towns were centers of Spanish culture and influence, far from the towns life continued much as it had for a thousand years.

Lahun Canche and his family lived in the forest in a clearing. He had wandered during the famine years and had seen men drop dead in the streets. He had lived for a time with the Spanish conquistadors and had moved back into the forest with his wife, sons, daughters, and their families. In the eastern provinces, the influence of the Spanish invaders was diluted, and here he lived under the tropical canopy. The message he sent out was clear. He dressed in a loincloth with a long cotton shirt and walked ramrod straight and as silent as the night. He carried a henequen bag and wore a few jade beads on a necklace and a bone passed through his nose. He was a symbol of Maya culture—tied to the past and, in a sense, contemptuous of the future. Most important to him was his family, and as head of his lineage and knowledgeable elder, he was responsible for rites and rituals binding the members of his family together and protecting them from evil spirits.

Lahun Canche looked out the doorway of his pole-and-thatch hut and passed through it as if it were a gateway to the forest beyond. It meant little to his younger sons, but to him the candles had to be burned on the stone before he felt at ease to hunt deer. He prayed to the sip *spirits to assist him, promised to take only those deer that were feeding in his field—and only enough to feed his family. With the prayer finished he stood tall again and moved to the forest to check his pitfall trap for the deer.*

He entered the cornfield and saw the cross that he had erected to protect his field from evil winds. A cross stood at each corner of the field and reminded him of the Bacab *who held up the four corners of the sky or the four* ceiba *trees or the four* Chacob. *He looked at the maize plants, and they were young and shimmering in the soft breeze and afternoon sun. They reminded him of the virile, young, and handsome Corn God. The chile bushes were healthy, and the fruits growing plump. He remembered planting them at the full moon with his wife and remembered the prayers they had chanted to the Moon Goddess. The spirits were all around him, teaching him to be alert to the forces under the tropical canopy.*

REVITALIZATION MOVEMENT (A.D. 1840–1920)

Francisco May marched south to Chan Santa Cruz with his wife, his brothers, and his young son, Silvestre. The family melted into the forest to escape from the federal forces and join the Cruzob forces to the east. The government forces seemed to be extraordinarily powerful, and it seemed as though only the gods could save the Maya. Under this cloud of doom, the Talking Cross of Chan Santa Cruz del Bravo evolved to revitalize the Maya and provide a vision of the future.

Walking along the forest paths, Francisco May was alert to the markers of the land. Here a deer had crossed the path, and there the old corn stalks marked an abandoned milpa. *Near the settlement of Chan Santa Cruz, Francisco came upon a cenote tucked deep within a rocky hill* (Bricker 1981, p. 103). *Nearby was a tiny cross carved into the trunk of a* ceiba *tree. This small holy cross became the focus of a revitalistic cult. The family entered the grotto with gourd containers and dipped out water to drink, refreshing themselves after their long journey. Entering the town of Chan Santa Cruz del Bravo, Francisco and his family saw that work was being done to build a stone church to house the Talking Cross. Here prophets would explain to the Maya that God himself commanded them to fight against the* dzulob, *or* blancos.

The *dzulob* attacked the shrine village in the 1850s and actually captured the Talking Cross and killed the ventriloquist, Manuel Nahuat, who spoke for the cross. When a new cross replaced the old one, with the help of Juan de la Cruz, it communicated in writing the outrageous treatment it received in the hands of its captors. The atrocities included stripping, peeling, and burning the flesh. Pesos, gold chains, chocolate, pigs, candles, horses, swords, pistols, and even 50 loads of corn were taken, robbed from the cross. These were tribute payments that the Indians had supplied. It was symbolic of what was taken from the Maya themselves by the *dzulob*.

As the Cult of the Talking Cross evolved, three men actually acted as leaders: One was a very old man who acted as secretary; another man acted as *Tatich* ("Patron of the Church and Talking Cross"), and a third young man acted as *Tata Naz* ("Speaker for the Talking Cross") and administered justice. The cross stood in the front of the church, *X Balam Na* (Jaguar House). Covered with a *huipil* or Indian woman's embroidered dress with a petticoat, the cross had an Indian identity. The cult mixed Mayan and European symbols from more than 200 years of interaction, but the Talking Cross talked to the Maya, not to the *dzulob*.

The cross talked at night, and the followers fell to the ground to hear the message. This duplicated the action that the *Chilam Balam* had followed when they entered trances hundreds of years earlier. Whoever acted as interpreter for the cross was acting in line with Maya traditions of prophetic announcements. Although these interpreters were from time to time killed by whites or even men of their own camps, replacements were found to translate the message of the Talking Cross. The scribes or secretaries also continued to report on the message of the cross far into the 1900s. The *Tatich, Nohoch Tata* ("Great Father"), and *Ah Kin* (High Priest) also survived into modern time. These keepers of knowledge saw to it that the altar was properly arranged with candles, incense, and other essential items. The cross still acts as intermediary between God and man. The situation in Quintana Roo is like that described by Bricker (1981, p. 113) for Chiapas: "Wherever a cross stands, there are the eyes of god."

Under the command of the Talking Cross, the Maya formed a military organization that acted to mobilize villagers for the Maya cause. Most of the soldiers were refugees from sections of the peninsula to the west who moved southeast to hide in the forest. One of the duties of the military men was to guard the religious temple. This tie between the Maya army and the temple of the Talking Cross united the Maya and gave the rebellion supernatural sanction.

In 1901, Francisco May watched the Mexican general Ignacio Bravo march with his troops into Chan Santa Cruz. Most of the town's people were gone, hiding in the forest. Francisco May was an elder and had stayed to negotiate with the invaders. The Mexican soldiers marched in to confront the old men in the plaza. The elders in their white pants, white shirts, and hemp sandals walked softly to meet the invaders. In their ears were elaborate gold earrings, a symbol of the *Tatichos*, religious leaders of the Cruzob. These old men, practitioners of rites that were thousands of years old, met with General Bravo and his federal troops. By 1915, the federal troops had withdrawn from Chan Santa Cruz after setting up a telegraph and telephone connection, a railway system, and a public water reservoir. All of these investments were torn down by the Maya as they effectively isolated themselves from the outside world.

TRADITION AND CHANGE (A.D. 1920–1985)

Don Silvestre May and his brothers were waking up in the early morning. They had been hunting the night before and today would cut rainforest to clear their fields. Their life under the tropical canopy connected them intimately with the natural world around them. Time repeated itself in cycles for these milperos. *Cut the forest, burn it, plant it, weed it, and harvest it. The agricultural cycle governed their sense of time. The sky could be read to determine whether the rains were coming, and whether the sun would blaze, and the length of the day could be determined by the sun and the shadows it made. The earth provided a wealth of information about seasonal time, time of day, other beings, and other resources.*

Silvestre May leaned back in his hammock and listened for a moment to the birds. He could see a vulture high up in a ramon *tree with its wings spread open to dry in the morning sun. Don Silvestre looked at the roof of the open-walled hut. Every batch of* guano *thatch was woven into a sapling frame with a series of crosses, and at the four corners of the shelter the upright* oracones *crossed with other limbs. The strong supports were like the* Bacab, *he thought, holding up the four corners of the world. He stood up and stretched his arms out, making a perfect picture of a cross with his own body, a perfect picture of the universe.*

He and his brothers began to cut the forest down to make a field for growing corn and other staples. Some large stones were encountered during the clearing, and the men set candles in front of the stones and prayed to the tun *spirits. Some* saca *(maize gruel) was offered. Later, when the sun had set and a small fire burned in the hut, Silvestre May reminded his brothers that they needed to provide offerings to the* alux *to ensure that they would guard their field. Don Silvestre began,*

"There once was a man who visited his field, and there he encountered two *alux*. They were dressed in blue pants with red jackets with a row of gold buttons. These *alux* had their tiny guns and their small dogs to help them. The farmer knew that the *alux* would protect his field, so he set up an altar and offered them *saca*. They accepted the drink, and the man made them a little house that he set up for them in his field. The *alux* guarded the man's field, and when deer came to rob him of his corn, the *alux* fired on the deer. Also, when a stranger came to hunt in the man's field, the *alux* fired their guns and the man ran away.

"Tomorrow," Don Silvestre said, "we will make offerings to the alux."

Time passed, and the fields were cut, burned, and planted. When the harvest was ready, Don Silvestre came to Coba with his family. They gathered the first fruits of the harvest (Figure 6.2). They dug a hole and filled the bottom with wood and rocks and fired it. After placing ears of corn in the hole, they covered them with leaves and buried them with earth. The pib, *or earth oven, cooked the corn overnight, and in the morning they opened the* pib *saying, "Open your mouth, Itzam. Ho, it is broken apart" (Roys 1965; pp. 49–50). With this, the earth monster opened the* pib *so that the people could enjoy the first corn. The family of Don Silvestre celebrated the good harvest and feasted on it. The corn was eaten on the cob taken hot from the* pib. *Other kernels had been finely ground and, with water and honey or salt, prepared as* atole, *a hearty drink served in* lecs, *or half gourds.*

After a few days had passed, Don Silvestre wanted to hunt. He gathered his sons together in the afternoon and told them this story to prepare them for the night.

Once there was a man who was living in Kanxoc. The man went hunting in the forest night after night. One night he was walking by a *milpa,* and he saw a deer. The man was alone, and when he looked again, there was another deer a little farther away. Suddenly, he heard a noise, and when he swung his lamp to his side, he saw that the forest was full of deer. This scared him, and he ran away. The next night, the man returned to hunt in the forest. Suddenly, he heard a noise coming toward him. He turned and ran, and the noise kept coming. All of the birds in the trees were squawking, and the man ran for 3 kilometers, and the noise followed him. He ran and ran, and the birds followed him squawking. Finally, he reached the village.

In the village, the night was very quiet. The man found his house, entered it, and lay down in his hammock. In the morning when he woke up, the man had a fever. He went to visit the *h-men,* who looked into his *sas* (crystal) to see what had given the man the sickness.

"What I see," said the *h-men,* "what I see in my *sas* is that the fever is not natural. The animals that you saw in the forest caused the fever, and this is why you are not well. If you had not run away, the animals would have eaten you.

Figure 6.2. "First Fruits" ceremony with songs and prayers, Coba.

What came to you was the king of the animals, and the king of the animals ran after you to eat you. But he did not catch you. Then he sent *mal viento* (an evil wind), and when you breathed this air, you got the fever.

"If you had not run, you would have died. The king of the animals was looking for you. You never sleep at night, you always look for deer. In the past, you went into the *monte* (forest) many times."

The *h-men* took *saca* and gave it to the man seven times; he also gave it seven times to his wife and seven times to his children. After seven times of taking *saca,* this grand ceremony of *Lolcatali* cured the man and changed his life. When the ceremony was finished, the *h-men* told the man never to go hunting in the forest again.

The *h-men* said, "If you go another time into the *monte,* you will not come out. The king of the animals, he will kill you. You have killed many animals, and you have bothered the animals of the *monte.* These animals have an owner. You passed across him."

The man never went into the *monte* again because he was afraid.

"My sons," Don Silvestre said, "Listen well to my story. We will hunt to-gether tonight but must offer candles and prayers to the king of the deer, the sip-iceh. *Take out of the forest only what you need."*

Don Silvestre and his sons hunted deer at night but did not hear or see a single one. Walking home, they passed the zapote *tree, and it had cuts down the trunk.*

"Ya, zac-ya, it is the trunk that gives itz *or resin. We cut* chicle *here around the lakes," Don Silvestre told his sons. "My brothers and I cut the trees, boiled the sap, and sold it in blocks at Puerto Morelos. Sometimes,* chicleros *put rocks in the center of the block or they put* masa *(corn dough) in the center. What a joke on the wealthy overseers." Don Silvestre smiled at the thought. "It is hard work cutting* chicle, *and in the small work camps isolated in the forest, strange happenings have been known to occur."*

Don Silvestre began another story to teach his sons:

In the *monte,* there was a *chiclero* camp. A woman and her daughter lived in the camp working as cooks. One day, the daughter crossed over the camp with a bucket to go and bathe. Suddenly, the girl screamed, and when her mother ran to look for her, she was gone. Only her clothes and the water bucket remained. Then the mother heard another scream, but very far away. The *chicleros* ran out to look for the girl, but they could not find her. They slept in the *monte* to wait for another cry, but they heard nothing. The girl's father went to get a *h-men,* and when they returned, the *h-men* tried to figure out what happened. The *h-men* said that the *dueño* of the forest, the *balam,* had taken the girl. The *balam* lived in a cave, and he had always lived there, but it was very hard to find. All of the *chicleros* went out to look for a cave near the area where the last scream was heard. They finally found the cave and saw the girl, but they stayed back. One *chiclero* went to get the *h-men,* and he came and began a ritual. The girl could not speak. She had been in the cave for four days. When her mother, father, and the *h-men* came close to her, the girl struck her mother. She had great strength, but they brought her back to camp. At nightfall, she still could not speak, nor could she sleep. The *h-men* prepared a ritual for the *dueño del monte,* the *balam.* When the ritual was over, the girl fell asleep. The next morning when she woke up, it was as though she were drunk. They gave her wine, *balche.* She had not eaten or drunk anything for four days. After this, she became well. She said that the apparition looked white, with white hair. This was the *balam.*

"The balam," *Don Silvestre told them, "guard the earth. They are pure air, like a jet, they come as wind."*

The next day, Don Silvestre and his grandson walked south to the rancho at Sinacal. Here he kept a few head of cattle. He had to check the beasts and make sure they had sufficient water. As they walked along the road, Don Silvestre told his grandson that he and the other men who had cattle at Sinacal were preparing to hold a ceremony, Los Corrales. *The little boy listened as his grandfather told him the story of X-Juan-Thul.*

"My child, if there passes a time when no rites are held for X-Juan-Thul, he

will kill all of the cattle in a corral and, sometimes, he will kill a child. If you do not perform the Los Corrales *ritual, X-Juan-Thul will kill or give sickness to members in the family. There is life in X-Juan-Thul."*

Long ago, there was a rich man who had many cattle. He had a wife and also a servant girl who lived in his house. The rich man liked the servant girl and had a child with her. "What am I going to do with the child," he thought. "What will my wife say? It is better to get rid of the child. I will throw the child in the path where my cattle walk. The child will be killed." So the rich man took the child and put it in the cattle path. Then he went to the *monte* to get the cattle, to run them so that they would stampede over the child. When the cattle were all gathered and the child was in the middle of the road, the cattle were stampeded, and all of them passed around the child. After the last cow had passed, the child ran into the forest and said this, "One day I will return to get revenge on my father because he did this evil act." After this happened, about a year passed, and all the man's cattle began to die. The *h-men* came and said that the sickness in the cattle was the son's revenge for what the father had done. The *h-men* said that the rich man should not be so preoccupied with material things. He said that the son now asked for part of his rich father's money. He wants a gift, an inheritance from you. The *h-men* told the rich man, "Give him this. Perform a rite in the corral for your son. If you don't do this, if you don't perform the ritual," the *h-men* said, "the child will kill all your cattle, and eventually, he will kill you, too. If you perform the ritual, only a few cattle will die, not all, and you will also be able to live."

"This is the reason that Los Corrales *started as a ceremony," said Don Silvestre. "It was for X-Juan-Thul. Although it is not now his father who is the owner of a corral, X-Juan-Thul will kill cattle and the owner will get sick if this ritual is not done. People invite a* h-men *to come to their new corral, and they cut a pole and put it in the middle of the corral. They cover it with a special leaf from the bottom to top. The leaves of* bobtun *are tied on the pole. Around the bottom of the pole they put* sacate. *On the* sacate, *they put* jicara *cups filled with* balche. *The* h-men *circles the pole seven times in one direction, drinking balche, and then seven times in the other direction in the same manner. Then the spirit of X-Juan-Thul enters the pole and protects the cattle. The cattle in the corral gather around the pole. There is another ceremony, an* acción de gracias *(thanksgiving ceremony) that you need to perform for the god who lives in the sky if you want to use land where an old corral was and if you want X-Juan-Thul to leave that place. My grandson, that is what your father had to do when he assumed ownership of his property where the old corral of Arturo Chimal used to be."*

The story ended, and Don Silvestre and his grandson had reached the rancho at Sinacal. Other men who owned cattle were checking their animals, and the elders begn to plan the Los Corrales *ceremony to protect their cattle, themselves, and their families.*

Don Silvestre was walking back from his cornfield with his sons and son-in-law, and they decided to take a rest on the rim of the Cenote de Venado. Sitting on a stone and smoking a cigarette, Don Silvestre told these stories about the evil spirit, xtabai.

Xtabai lives in cenotes or in caves in the *monte*. She is a serpent that appears as a beautiful woman. One time in the nearby town of Chemax, there were various *xtabai* who came and found drunks. They appeared to these men in the form of their wives. They would take the men by the hand and lead them out of town.

One time, *xtabai* took a man to the mouth of a cave and told him it was his house. "Jump," she cried, "jump through the door." But the drunk saw that if he jumped he would go into a cenote in the cave. Then he started to yell. There were houses nearby, and the men from these ran to see what was wrong. The man told them that a woman had brought him to the edge of the cenote. They all agreed that it was *xtabai*. This was very dangerous. If he had jumped, he would have died.

Another time, there was a young man who went to visit his *novia* (girlfriend) at about 9:00 at night. When he arrived at her house, his girlfriend was standing in the entrance. The young man thought that she was waiting for him. He talked to her, and she answered back. "Let's go to my house," he said, and off they went. Finally, they arrived at the edge of the pueblo. "Why are we going this way?" he said. She took his hand; and her hand was ice cold, and she had no thumb. He realized that this was not his girlfriend, and he began to yell. She pulled him into the forest, and she was very strong. He grabbed at tree trunks, first small ones, and she tugged him away. Then he wrapped his arms around a great big trunk. She pulled at him, she ran around the tree to get him free. All this time, the young man was yelling. The people knew that *xtabai* was around, and when they heard the young man yelling, they ran to see what it was. When they arrived, the woman let go of his hand and disappeared. The men looked for her, but she was gone. The young man's clothes and his arms were covered with thorns.

"If there is no acción de gracias, *you will see a woman appear with long white hair, and this is* xtabai. *She can take the form of a woman or a goat. When people are a little bit drunk, they may have the strength or valor to touch* xtabai. *If you throw stones at her, she will go away, but the person will get sick with a fever. People say that* xtabai *will bother people and that* xtabai *can stand on the outside wall of a house near a person who has bothered her. She will throw a lasso into the house, and it will go around your legs and give you a sickness. You can be cured but need a* h-men. *If you bother* xtabai *or if you are bothered by her, you have to go to a* h-men *to perform a rite over the sickness and over* xtabai *to cure the illness and to confuse* xtabai *so that she will behave and leave you alone.*

"Xtabai sometimes also appears as a snake called chakan, *a green and yellow snake.*

There was a young man who had an evil heart, and he would grab women. One time, there was a beautiful woman combing her long hair sitting near a *ceiba* tree, and the young man grabbed her. It was *xtabai,* and she changed into a green and yellow snake. The young man fell over, and the snake wrapped around his body. *Xtabai* rolled with him and took him over the mouth of a cenote, and there he died.

"Xtabai is a spirit, a bad spirit that roams in the night. Xtabai can change

forms, and when you are drunk, you think it is your mother, your father, your brother, or your girlfriend. But is is xtabai *who has come to take you and kill you.''*

By this time, everyones' eyes were wide with fear. It was getting to be late afternoon, and the light beneath the tree canopy cover was dim. The men looked into the dark cave where the cenote was hidden in the shadow. They shivered, stood up, and began their walk back to the center of town.

The cornfield is of central importance to the Maya villager and, in fact, is itself a model of the Maya universe. It is in the *milpa* that the sky, earth, and underworld meet and man acts as mediator. From a natural forest of wild plants and animals, the field is transformed into a culturally defined space inhabited by supernatural forces like *tun* (spirits in stones), *alux* (dwarf-tricksters), *sipiceh* (master of the deer), and the *balam* (owner of the forest). The health and productivity of the field relies most heavily on the vagaries of rain. If it does not rain, corn seeds shrivel and fail to germinate. If it pours, the beans trail along the ground, and the moisture rots the vines and turns the crop into a rotting soup. Also, the squash flowers are detached from the vines by hard rains and fail to form fruit. Later in the season, heavy winds snap the corn stalks, and the entire crop will be lost. The actions that have been taken to mitigate these crises are petitions and offerings to the mighty and ancient Rain Gods, the *Chacob*. The thunder is the running horse and the lightning is the sword of the *Chacob*.

The forest had been cut down, dried, and fired. After the ground had cooled, Don Silvestre and his sons began to plant nal *(corn) and* buul *(beans). They walked over the cleared* milpa *with a bag full of mixed seed, and with digging stick, they poked holes where the soil was deep enough and dropped in the seeds. With the ground full of seed, the men waited anxiously for the rains.*

Silvestre May sat with his sons in their milpa, *sheltered from the sun beneath the thatched roof of the* nainal *(corn storage hut). The* elotes *(corn plants) were half a meter high and fluttered in the breeze. The rains were slight, and Don Silvestre told his sons, "It is time to hold a rite to petition the* Chacob *to bring rain." Don Silvestre told his son, Jose Asuncion, to ask the men of other families to help them sponsor the ceremony.*

Jose Asuncion, Arturo Chimal, Elusio Cuyoc, Alonso Cen, Felipe Chan, and Teodoro May walked out of town to the west to Chac Ne, *the rancho of Demetrio Pol, the* h-men. *They asked him if he would perform the* Chachac *ceremony, and he agreed to do so. It is the old people who know how to do this ceremony. Younger people do not understand it or do not know how to do it. The six men made their plans for the* Chachac.

Eight days before the ceremony, the men went off into the forest to hunt for a deer. In the milpa *of Don Silvestre, they shot one and carried it back to the village. They dried and cooked the meat on a* chache *rack over a fire. A few days before the ceremony, Jose Asuncion and Teodoro May prepared the ceremonial* balche. *They cut the bark off the* balche *trunk and cooked the bark* (Figure 6.3). *Three times they cooked the bark in new water. The bark was set in the sun to dry for four days. The day before the ceremony, they placed the bark in a* pila

Figure 6.3. Jose Isabel Cocom collecting the bark of the balche *tree for making wine.*

(trough) of cedar and added three buckets of water and 5–6 kilograms of honey. A few grains of anise and cinnamon were stirred into the mixture. When this was done, a cover was placed over the pila. The next day, when foam appeared, the balche was ready.

On the day of the ceremony, the sponsors gathered in front of the pyramid in *the Ruins of Coba. They made a table from saplings, and across the table, they constructed arches made from* ximche *branches covered with green leaves. Away from the corners of the table, four arches were constructed on the ground. These represented the four winds that blow in from the four cardinal directions. In the morning, they excavated a big hole for a* pib *or earth oven to cook* nohua *or corn cakes.*

The Chachac *ceremony started in the late afternoon. Three* jicaras *(gourd cups) were hung from the arches on the altar, twelve cups were placed on the table on leaves of* habin, *and one cup was placed beneath the table on a* habin *leaf. The* jicaras *were filled with* saca.

Away from the table, other men were making the nohua *and constructing the* pib. *The hole was filled with saplings from the* habin *tree, and stones were set over these. The fire was started, and the stones turned red hot. The men patted out* gordas *(large, thick tortillas) and covered these with ground squash seeds. Seven* gordas *were piled up and set onto the hot rocks. In the middle of the* pib, *a bucket full of* masa *was set, and the* gordas *surrounded this. Leaves of* bobtun *were placed over this, and then the fan-shaped thatch leaves of* guano. *The oven was covered with soil, and the* nohua *cakes began to slowly cook.*

Don Demetrio stood at the altar and held the saca. *He said the rosaries in place. The* h-men *sang and repeated rosary after rosary. He drank the* saca. *A drink of* arroz *(rice) was poured into the* jicara, *and the* h-men *began his recitations once again. Chocolate was poured into the* jicara *and* saca *was poured again. These offerings and recitations continued through the night. Through the night, the* h-men *sang rosaries calling and asking the saints and the* Chacob *to bring the rains.*

In the very early morning before dawn, the men placed venison in a large pot, and chicken was placed in a separate large cook pot. To these, they added water, masa, *garlic, and pepper. These stews, or soups were cooked until late morning.*

Don Demetrio was red eyed and tired. He had recited through the night to call the Chacob. *He sat quietly on a small* caanche *(cedar bench) and watched the other men open the* pib *and draw out the* gordas. *Portions of the cooked* masa *were placed in the stew, and portions were placed over the altar. Don Demetrio stood up and walked to the altar. He began to sing. Away from the table stood an old man who held a* lelem *(sword), a large* chu *(hard squash shell), and a small* calabaza *(squash shell) filled with* balche. *This man was the* Chac *impersonator. The old man blew into the* chu, *and the noise of* Chac *resounded. He moved his sword, and it was the lightning of the* Chac. *Don Demetrio sang, and the* Chac *impersonator responded. The table was prepared by Don Demetrio, and he found four young boys, whom he led to the table. They squatted down at the four corners and made noises like frogs, harbingers of the rain. The* h-men *sang, and the* Chac *impersonator laughed and "talked" through his* calabaza. *The* h-men *sang, "Come, come, oh* Chacob," *and the "Chac" passed close to the table. He was offered* balche, *and the children sang and Don Demetrio sang.*

The h-men *tasted the cooked* masa *from the table, and all the men who had attended the ceremony approached the altar and ate the cooked corn dough. The* h-men *passed his* sas *crystal over the candle on the table and asked,*

"Where are the rains? Where are the Chacob?*" He then announced that it would rain in three days. The ceremony was over. People were given pieces of* gorda *and then stew to eat. The* h-men *went to touch the* nohua *and the stew of each person. People then wandered off to their houses.*

Three days later, the sky darkened and the rains rolled in from the east. The Chacob *whips cracked as lightning struck with a clash. The* Ah-lelem-caan-chac *rolled across the sky (the* Chac *with lightning). Don Demetrio stood in the doorway of his rancho. Just before the rains fell, he looked out, and the tree branches swayed, twisted and turned in the wind. He thought to himself, "Here come the* Chacob, *pure wind,* viento, ik.*" He entered his house, and because of the thunderclouds, the enclosure was as dark as a cave. He lit a candle and squatted by the hearth near his wife's side. She dipped a* lec *into the pot and offered him some stew and handed him a portion of* nohua, *the* gorda *with* pepita *seeds. To his side, she placed a cup of coffee sweetened with sugar. The* h-men *and his wife ate the ceremonial food and stared out the door at the falling rain.*

CONCLUSION

From the very beginning of time, the Maya inhabited a world with many spirits. In the epoch of the ancient ones, even wood and stone had spirits. The Maya were able to collect firewood by whistling, for the wood (leña) would walk itself home. Stones, as well, would enter a yard and, climbing on top of each other, miraculously build a house. Until man himself carried wood home and piled up stone, breaking the magic, the spirits enhanced the life of the ancestors.

The supernatural world of the Maya was built on dualistic principles, perhaps the most obvious of which is the dual quality of the gods—both benevolent and malevolent. The *Chac* Rain Gods, for example, could water seed, cause it to germinate, and encourage its growth, or they could be ferocious and destroy the crop. Corn harvest time and hurricane time coincided on the east coast of Yucatan.

The complicated hierarchy of supernatural beings makes it clear that the Maya were extraordinarily focused on religion and magic but that certain deities served certain sectors of the population. The priestly elite in pre-Columbian times were concerned with a Venus Cult, for example, and traders prayed and petitioned *Ek Chuah*. *Milperos* focused on the good graces of the Corn God, the *Chac* Rain Gods, the spirits that inhabited stones in their fields, and the *alux* who could protect their crops from intruders.

The invasion of the peninsula by the Spaniards was cataclysmic for the Maya. Political domination stripped the traditional society not only of the *batabs* (governors) but of the contributions at the highest levels of the religious hierarchy. The high priests and high political officers had combined the roles of politics and religion. The priest-rulers were the intellectuals of the society. With their positions obliterated, the focus of traditional religion was earthly, concerned with agricultural deities, spirits of the field and forest.

During the Caste War (1840–1920), religion was used to revitalize Maya

Figure 6.4. Milpa *fields surrounded by forest.*

society. The movement of the Talking Cross provided supernatural sanction to military resistance to federal forces. Incredibly, the Maya succeeded in repulsing intrusion into the eastern sector of Yucatan until the territory of Quintana Roo became a state in 1974. With the construction of roadways, the bringing in of electric lines, and the massive development of the tourism industry on the eastern coast, the old system began to fray. The old rites that had been performed in *milpa,* in corrals, for bees, for the *Chac* Rain Gods, and for the protection of families and villages were rarely performed or by only a few families.

The village of Coba has become a meeting place for the ancient and the modern. The elders have lived and continue to live a traditional pattern that includes the practice of rituals that protect man and the land by evoking supernatural attention. On the other hand, the young men, heads of new families, despite having heard of the spirits and rituals, do not believe in them and have never seen most of the traditional rites performed.

Far from the center of the village, Nicolas Caamal rested in his hammock under a thatched hut or nainal. *The wall-less structure permitted a perfect view of his* milpa *and being set up on a rise, allowed him to view the forest on all four sides of his field* (Figure 6.4). *It was a beautiful afternoon, and Nicolas relaxed eating a watermelon. His son sat on a rush mat near his head. Inquisitive, the boy asked about the squawking birds, and his father told him which birds were singing. They watched two heavy-nosed toucans sail across the field near the forest trees. The boy asked his father about the land. Nicolas pointed out the areas where the soil was deep and fine for planting corn and the exposed bedrock areas that were good for setting up a* nainal.

"The big stones are tun," *he told his son. "Put candles and* saca *before them and make an offering when you plant."*

The afternoon was over and the sun slipped below the horizon. The father lit a fire, and they ate some fat gordas *that Maria, his wife, had prepared for them in the morning. As it became dark, the boy heard a noise and shivered with fear.*

"That is the alux, *my son. Do not fear them. I have offered* saca *to these guardians of my* milpa."

The father laid the young boy in the hammock and covered him with a thin blanket. As the boy fell into dreams, the man stared out into the darkness and he heard the trees bend and rustle as the wind passed through them. "It is the balam," *he whispered to himself. He curled up on the mat near the fire and fell asleep—as had the Maya farmer for thousands of years, surrounded by spirits that had been petitioned and, on this night, meant him no harm.*

7/Tradition and Change

PRE-HISPANIC PERIOD (A.D. 600–900)

While the climax rainforest is a high canopy with an open, sunless floor—peaceful and beautiful, the low rainforest closes in with smaller saplings, thickets and a woven barrier of vines. The world of nature is thorny— the underbrush is a tangled web, grabbing at your feet, whipping across your face, and catching in your hair. A cleared area in a rainforest is a bed of fallen saplings, with a springboard effect—treacherous to traverse. It lies drying in the sun, prepared to fire, to enrich the thin soil with wood ash. When it cools down, it is ready for planting. The planted field is a man-made clearing full of corn, beans, and squash. The vines of root crops thread along the floor, and chile pepper bushes grow in the hot, tropical sun nourished by the rains. The fat papaya hang from branches, and mandarin oranges shine in the sun. Bunches of bananas ripen on the tall plants. The green leaves of corn plants glisten in the sun, fluttering in the slightest breeze. After the harvest, the corn stalks dry out and turn brown. The abandoned field fills with grasses and other weeds. Small saplings grow up as thin stalks, and the area is transformed again into a natural world.

It was this world of nature that the Maya became so expert in decoding. From ancient times, the Maya studied the natural world—observing it, testing it, and learning to utilize its resources in ways that became uniquely Mayan. For example, the *subin* tree, covered with biting ants, has thorns that can be used as needles to remove splinters. *Anicab* vines, a nuisance when they cross your path, can be pulled up in lengths of 5, 10, or more meters and used in house building—to tie tree trunks for framing the walls or to tie saplings for framing the roof. The vines also can be used—for making baskets for storage or for collecting *elote* (ripe corn) from the field. A flat plate of woven vine (*peten*) can be easily made and hung from house rafters to protect food from being eaten by rats. The resources of the high rainforest include valuable resins, hardwoods for making furniture, and smaller plants used for concocting herbal medicines. The cleared rainforest of fallen timbers is a useful source of firewood for the hearth, fertilizer for the *milpa*, and space for growing food. The *milpa* is a miniature reflection of the natural forest—full of many species of plants, wild and cultivated, essential for life itself. However, the land can be farmed only a short time before it needs a rest to regenerate. A few years of cultivation is the limit, and then the field must be allowed to revert back to forest. The men turn from the old plot to new forest land to make a living.

The Farmer

Far from the center of the city, the Maya farmer woke up in the very early morning. He could hear the birds singing and looking out the doorway, he saw a vulture perched high in a ramon tree with its black wings spread open to dry in the morning sun. The air was cool, and the farmer wrapped a cotton cape around his shoulders. He could hear his wife moving behind him, and he accepted a container full of steaming chocolate from her. He sipped at the scalding liquid and began to plan the day ahead. He had cleared his milpa plot in the high rainforest and burned the dry brush. The soil was covered with wood ash, and he had planted his corn and beans with a digging stick when his father's brother told him the time was auspicious. His uncle was a rainmaker, and they had held a ceremony to petition the curled-nosed Chacob to push the clouds over the field and bring the rains.

The corn had ripened, and the beans began to grow up around the stong cornstalks. The farmer had also planted squash to shade the roots of the corn and beans and keep the weeds down. Nearby, he planted chile, and in the bottom of an old cenote, he planted cacao trees. Today he would check his milpa and carry back some dried elote (corn) from his nainal (storage house). His harvest had been good for two seasons, and he held a ceremony of thanksgiving offering the first fruits of his harvest to the gods. His father's brother would travel to his milpa with him on this day. The elder would collect medicinal plants in his milpa, in his abandoned field, and along the forest trail. The old man was a curer, a h-men, and he needed to prepare remedies for hubnak (diarrhea). It was a rainy season, and many members of the family had fallen ill, especially the small children. The elder was looking for chacal-haaz (the fruit of the mamey tree) or on (avocado) to prepare his remedy.

The farmer, his father's brother, and his young son finished their chocolate and left the house. They walked along the path through the forest. The young boy jumped up on limestone boulders, skipped over the vines that crossed the path, ducked under branches, and searched for tepescuintli (small rodents) as the men silently walked along (Figure 7.1). When they arrived at the farmer's milpa, they walked across to the nainal, and the elder sat down to rest. The farmer picked up a gourd and headed for the cenote to get some water. He had good luck with this field. The cenote held clear, clean water through the dry season. He dipped the gourd into the cool water and waited for it to fill. The farmer walked back to the thatch-covered lean-to and offered the old man some water. After they had rested, the old man took a corn cob from the pile and went with the farmer to collect the fruits. Meanwhile, the young boy had filled his little henequen bag with chile peppers to bring back home to his mother. After the farmer had helped collect the fruit, he loaded a large henequen sack with corn and, with a tumpline across his forehead, lifted the load onto his back. The three started

Figure 7.1. Young boy holding a tepescuintli.

home, walking along the path through the forest. The farmer had checked his field, his son had finished his work, and the old man had collected the substances he needed to prepare his herbal remedies. In the middle of the day, the men walked along the path in the shade under the closed canopy of the high tropical forest. Occasionally, they would climb up onto one of the sacbeob *(elevated limestone roads) and walk along its plastered surface. But the sun was high in the sky and hot, so they frequently stepped off the road and went back into the shaded forest.*

The Family

Articulation with the natural world for the Maya entailed social interaction and cooperation. The most obvious social unit among the Maya was the family. Its organization varied from small nuclear families to large extended family groups. The function of the family was not unlike that of families everywhere, including the care and enculturation or teaching of children. The family supplied economic support to its members. Power was allocated by age and sex, and the family unit participated in rites of passage (birth, marriage, and death ceremonies) and other religious rituals for the welfare of themselves and other members of the village. For the Maya and other tropical farmers, the composition and organization of the family provided an essential labor force to enhance the economic livelihood of the group. Young male members assisted the elder men in making *milpa*, planting orchards, and caring for bees. Young female members of the family assisted the elder women in preparing food, washing clothes, running errands, and caring for small children. The family members, both young and old, were individually unique but operated in social union for the welfare of the entire unit.

The family was a clearly defined unit demarcating who belonged in the group and who did not. The wall between insiders and outsiders was more than a psychological barrier. The houselot wall gave the family its distinct boundaries.

The farmer, his son, and his father's brother finally arrived at home. The farmer dropped his bag of corn near the house and squatted down in the shade of the wall to rest. The boy offered his bag of chile to his mother without a word, and she accepted it with pride. She knew that the boy was excited to begin working with his father, and she smiled as the son went to sit in the shade by his father. She slipped inside the house and dipped into the large ceramic container where she kept drinking water. Inside the house, the porous clay vessel kept the water cool. She brought some water to her husband, and he shared it with the boy. After they had rested and finished their drink, she asked them if the old man had collected his medicine. Her youngest child had hubnak, *and she needed the medicine for the baby. She had heard the wailing from her neighbor's house and had known that it meant a child of that household had died in the night. She knew that the family had dug a hole and buried the child under the floor of the house.*

She looked around the household compound. Within these boundaries lived the family that she depended on for her welfare and the security of her children. Her husband's father and his wife lived in the largest house. Her husband's father's brother was the rainmaker, the curer, the h-men, *and lived in a smaller house. How lucky they were to have him in their family. He was the keeper of knowledge and protected not only their family but their neighbors. Nearby was the house of her husband's older brother and his wife. His wife was her older sister, and she was glad to have a member of her own family nearby. Her own nuclear family lived in the smallest house—herself, her husband, her son, and her baby. She knew that she was pregnant again, and this brought great joy. She hoped that she might give birth to a baby girl this time. She looked forward to having a girl to teach, and eventually, the girl would help her make clothes and prepare* tortillas. *She was content, and the family, both young and old members, depended on her contributions to enhance the welfare of the entire unit.*

The day became the night, and the supernatural forces—the ik, *winds that traveled anywhere they wished—blew through the compound. At night, the* ik *would cross the paths of unsuspecting victims and inflict them with sickness. People covered themselves, especially their heads, for protection.*

Mother, Child, and H-men

The sound that woke the woman in the night was her baby whimpering. The hut was dark, and she crawled toward the infant. She felt for the baby and could smell the foul odor. She lifted the child and offered him her breast, but the baby was too weak to feed. The woman stood up and wrapped a cloak around her shoulders, over her head, and covered the baby in her arms. She walked out the door and crossed the yard. She could see a candle burning in the house of the curer. How had he heard the child? She entered his hut, and he reached for the infant. He had already prepared the medicine and pressed it into the child's mouth. The old man had boiled water, and it had been sweetened with honey. It was only warm now, and he gently encouraged the baby to sip the liquid from the cup. He pressed medicine made from corn meal and the fruit of the chacal-haaz *into the baby's mouth, then water, and more medicine. In a very low voice, he instructed the woman on what to do to try and cure the baby. The woman took the medicine and the warm liquid and slipped out the door with her baby. For the rest of the night, she fed the baby the medicine and the warm liquid.*

When the sun came up in the morning, the baby was still alive. The woman's sister entered the house and took the baby while the woman started the fire and, on a clay griddle, warmed tortillas. *She put the water for chocolate over the fire. Over the fire, within the three sacred stones, the woman offered a prayer of thanksgiving to* Ix Chel, *Goddess Protector of Coba, for the life of her baby.*

THE COLONIAL PERIOD (A.D. 1539–1810)

The family provided a security net for individuals. Children were raised within the family and taught about the world they lived in by parents, older siblings, and grandparents. Storytelling was one way the young learned and were captured by their culture. The variety of folktales guided individuals to follow one path or another. Family ties extended far beyond the household group, binding the individual to other households in the village by kin or marriage and to villages scattered across the peninsula. Young men worked in *milpas* with their fathers-in-law, and young women sat around hearths bending over *comals* (griddles) making *tortillas* with their mothers-in-law, mothers, sisters, and daughters. Exchanges were made between kin and among friends. In the small-scale society, kinship and friendships encouraged human interaction.

The Farmer and the H-men

Lahun Canche was working with his sons in the milpa. *They had cut the forest and let it dry. They had set the* milpa *on fire, and the flames had reached higher than the tree tops. One section of forest had burned until the living trees stopped the blaze. Now, the forest was dry, waiting for the rains to turn it green again. Now, the men inspected their work. The fire had burned all of the brush and most of the large tree limbs and trunks. The wood ash covered the ground. They had invited an* h-men *to perform a ritual to cool the earth, and they walked with him around the field. Lahun watched the sky for clouds that would mark the coming of the rainy season. He could see black smoke rising in the air. The other ranchers were also burning their* milpa *plots. He was surprised to see so much smoke, so much more than when he first came into this part of the forest. He re-membered when he first brought his family into the eastern province. He would climb up on the mounds around the lake zone and could see smoke in the dis-tance, far from his* rancho. *Now, he could easily see the smoke from the ground as more families moved into the eastern area to escape the* dzulob. *As more peo-ple moved into the area, the rains were less apt to fall as heavy. He was sure that conditions were drier now than when he first settled in the area. "Too much fire," he thought to himself. "The fire is drying out the whole rainforest."*

Shaking his head, he turned to see the h-men *performing his ritual and no-ticed that the old man's grandson was kneeling by the altar leaning lightly against the* h-men. *He saw his own grandson standing nearby. The boy held a digging stick for planting corn and a henequen bag hung over his shoulder for the seed. The two young boys were already beginning to follow the path of their elders. He knew that the* h-men *had sons and that these boys had married. Their wives had children, and Lahun Canche began thinking that a marriage tie with the family of a* h-men *would be an important connection.*

Society, Economy, and Ritual

The Maya adjusted to the small-scale life on ranchos by promoting social ties. Collection of goods and the redistribution of items (particularly food) was an economic pattern that enhanced security for all families living under the tropical canopy. While one family might be lucky and have a large har-vest one year, another year the vagaries of rainfall and the force of the burn-ing sun might spoil a crop—or a whole harvest might be lost. The economic web that collected and centralized goods and redistributed the excess en-sured that no one starved. This redistribution of economically important goods was formalized under ritual circumstances that traditionally occurred throughout the yearly cycle. Rituals provided a setting for food redistribu-tion and economic security for all. Ritual celebrations also provided a setting for cementing social ties, creating social obligations, reinforcing social re-sponsibilities, and setting up social privileges. Economic well-being in the rainforest was not an easy achievement.

The Harvest

Lahun Canche had a successful harvest with the assistance of his sons. He harvested his corn and stored it in the nainal *in the* milpa, *and he hauled the beans home. Here in the yard area, the women of his household removed the beans from the pod and packed them in henequen bags. The women laid the chile out in the sun to dry. The* rancho *was a self-sufficient unit when the har-vest was good. When the harvest failed, the family had to rely on social ties to help them.*

One morning while the men were preparing to leave for work in the milpa *and gather some corn to bring back to the family compound, the old* h-men *stopped by to visit. They offered him some chocolate, and he sat down on a low seat carved out of cedar. The old man looked painfully thin, his cheeks were sunken, and his flesh hung on his old bones. He sipped at his chocolate and finally he spoke.*

"My friends," he began, "my family has had a terrible year. The insects have eaten our crops, the sun has baked the ground and ruined the corn, and the rain and winds have destroyed the beans. I have come to offer you my services for a thanksgiving ceremony. Perhaps, if I offer my services to you, you may offer some of your surplus to my family."

Lahun looked at his old friend. "Nohoch tata, old grandfather, thank you for reminding us that we should have a thanksgiving ritual. If you would perform the service for us we would be grateful. We have surplus corn, and my sons will carry the bags on their backs to your rancho. Tell us what you need, and we will send it to your house. I only ask one other favor. My grandson needs a wife who will work hard, and we will treat her as our own daughter. If you would agree to sending one of your granddaughters to become my grandson's wife, we would be willing to send more corn to your rancho to express how grateful we are." The old man nodded his assent to this plan. Lahun Canche believed that this would achieve his goal.

Lahun Canche walked along a path in the forest to his milpa. He was thinking about the marriage of his grandson to the granddaughter of the h-men. It would be a very important tie between the two families. He reached his milpa and stood on the perimeter looking across the cleared land. Suddenly, he heard a rattle and, looking down, saw a snake strike at his ankle. The fangs pierced his flesh, and the snake's venom entered his blood stream. The snake was so fat and long it could barely move, but the man had disturbed it, and the snake defended itself in the only way it knew how. Lahun moved slowly and looked for the herb xcambalhau. He saw the herb, broke off the stem, and let the white sap run into his mouth. It was bitter. He knew that he must not move, and he kept taking the healing sap from the stem of the herb. Perhaps his sons would pass by or his wife might come by collecting firewood. Lahun felt very weak, he wanted to close his eyes and sleep, but he kept taking the medicine. The next morning, his sons found him laying in the path to the milpa. Lahun Canche was dead, but his plan for his family had been completed. They dug a hole in the floor of the house and buried him. They put a stone ax by his side, a pot with some kernels of maize near his head, and an obsidian blade with the burial. The family abandoned the house and moved deeper into the forest.

MODERN PERIOD

Don Silvestre was working with his son in his milpa. It was early morning, and they were cutting the small saplings—preparing the field to make a space for the field to be planted. Don Silvestre was chopping at a larger sapling with a steel ax, and the ax slipped. It set the old man off balance, and he fell into the cut timbers. His head struck a trunk, and he lost consciousness. Jose Asuncion saw his father fall and ran to his aid. The old man lay still as though he were

sleeping. The son saw the red mark on his father's temple. He could see move-
ment in his father's chest and knew that he was alive. The son ran for the water
jug and gently wiped his father's face with the cool water. Eventually, the old
man opened his eyes and grasped his son's arm. "My son," he softly whispered,
"I can't see. I'm blind." The son helped his father along the path back to his
house. There, the old man was led to a hammock to rest while his son rushed to
find the h-men. When the curer examined Don Silvestre, he saw that there was
no cure for this illness.

Don Silvestre was an old man when he became blind. He had taken a second
wife; his sons and daughters who lived near his house were married and had chil-
dren of their own. The family provided Don Silvestre with his food. His wife had
fruit trees around their house and a kitchen garden. The grandchildren gathered
around the old man, and he would tell them stories about the Caste War and
Kanxoc, the Tatich *at Chan Santa Cruz, the* alux, tun *spirits,* X-Juan-Thul, *and*
the sorceress, xtabai. *He was the storyteller, and the history and legends of the*
culture were transmitted from him to the subsequent generation. His family,
blood kin, relatives by marriage, and compadres *ensured the security of Don*
Silvestre and tied him and his family into social, economic, and ritual obliga-
tions. Although blinded, Don Silvestre saw clearly into the past, and the patterns
of the past were suitable for living life under the tropical rainforest until the very
end of this old man's life.

Making *milpa* is arduous work. Although it is the way to begin, most men
try to invest some of their energies in other directions to minimize their work
in the cornfields. Investing in beehives and cattle, planting orchards or
kitchen gardens, cushion the economic uncertainty of *milpa* cultivation. For
as population density increases, a long rest and rejuvenation period for the
forest plots becomes impossible. With shorter fallow periods, the harvest
yields fall short. Without the high rainforest to enhance moisture regime re-
tention, the ecological setting becomes progressvely drier, and minor
changes in rainfall become major problems.

The Maya are preoccupied with monitoring rainfall as their very lives de-
pend on a precise regimen of moisture. Without the rains, the crops wither
and die. The rainforest is disappearing in the Yucatan, and with its disap-
pearance, the chances for success in *milpa* production are slim. For centuries the Maya have sought the virgin forest, moving away from congested
areas into the *monte* (jungle) to hunt, cut *chicle*, and ultimately, to farm. In
the 1980s, the Maya reached the limits of their frontier. The possibilities for
economic success in *milpa* agriculture have become sharply limited, and
economic life under the tropical canopy is being drastically modified (Figure
7.2).

Nicolas Caamal renounced his membership in the Coba ejido, along with
several other men. Making milpa *around the Coba lakes was not as successful*
as in earlier years. The high rainforest had been cut down, and the ejido *was*
mainly low rainforest, abandoned milpas, *and newly cut fields. The harvests*
failed, and people were sure that the rains were coming less frequently than in
their grandfather's time. Nicolas and several men of the village had organized

Figure 7.2. Young girl looks into the future.

to form a new ejido *in national forest lands. In high rainforest, perhaps the* milpas *would be more productive.*

Farming in the High Rainforest

In the late afternoon, Nicolas rode his bicycle out to check his new milpa. *One of his fields was located right off the main road. He dropped his bike and walked across this field to drop his supplies in his* nainal, *and then he set out through the forest to another area located away from the road. This field was surrounded by forest where deer and other wild animals would come to feed. Nicolas had come to hunt these animals. He could see the spoor of deer, and he climbed a tree to wait. He had brought an old* tortilla *and chewed it as he waited. As the sun dropped below the horizon, Nicolas heard a deer rustle the brush, and he slowly turned to see it enter his field. The doe moved cautiously, and behind her was a newly born fawn. Raising his rifle, Nicholas took aim, and the shot rang out. The doe collapsed, and the tiny fawn shivered and slowly approached its dead mother. Nicolas climbed down from the tree and approached the tiny creature. He slipped a rope over the fawn and tied it to a sapling. He tied the doe to his back, lifted the tiny fawn into his arms, and began his trek out to the main road. He flagged a truck down, and the trucker helped him lift the doe into the back of the truck. Nicolas climbed into the truck holding the fawn in his lap.*

Returning home, Nicolas hung the deer up and drained the blood. Next he dug a hole and loaded it with wood and rocks. In this subterranean oven, the venison would be cooked. He butchered the doe, sold some of the meat, and placed the rest in the oven. Covering the meat with leaves and sealing the oven with soil, he rested and waited for the time to open the oven and begin the feasting on the deer meat. He was lucky to have the deer. As the human population increased, the animal population decreased. The tiny fawn was tied to a sapling, and his children petted it and played with it.

Tradition and Change

On the village level, the basic organizational unit is the family. It is the family that regulates the use of space and access to resources and reinforces status positions. Informally, from day to day, the family guides, cajoles, and forces its members to perform essential tasks. The elders assume positions of authority, children mimic the same-sex parent, and life goes on. On the village level, elders assume positions as mediators or negotiators when a conflict arises. After the conflict is resolved, the mediator returns to the normal activities of farming, beekeeping, and cattle raising.

Political life on the village level has been informal and situational, and in the small-scale society, this political form was adequate. However, as population grew and the size of the village doubled, structural changes in political organization were initiated. The mayor of the village no longer farmed, and the president of the *ejido* was a rich beekeeper with no *milpa*. A full-time policeman prowled the town, and a new and substantial jail was built. These changes and investments legitimized the power of the politicians and their attendants. In the early days, very few outsiders visited the village of Coba. In 1972 a small group of archeologists began to survey the ancient stones, and by the 1980s, busloads of people were coming in from the outside to visit the archeological site. The small-scale and isolated nature of the village had changed, and regulations were becoming more common, controlling the lives of the residents of Coba. The informal consensus was changing to formal coercion.

Life in the village was far from repressive and had the facade of continuing the same as before, but minor changes were cracking the picture of life that had existed for thousands of years.

The Maya had resisted control from outsiders and maintained their culture under the tropical canopy. The ancient Itza invasion was diluted by the strength of the Maya culture. The political stratagems of the Maya (the Xiu, Chel, and Canul) in the 1400s at Mayapan destroyed the Cocom reign of power. The Spanish attempts to govern the Maya succeeded to some extent in the towns but failed miserably in the outlying villages that remained isolated from the rules and regulations inhibiting traditional Maya culture. Under pressure from the Spanish overlords, the eastern Maya slipped back into the forest and were able to live independent lives on *ranchos*—farming, bee keeping, raising cattle, and organizing politically into small, autonomous and independent families.

For centuries after the Spaniards entered the peninsula, the forest canopy prevented political domination of the Maya. In the 1850s, the Maya rebelled against economic and political pressure by outsiders (ladinos, and *dzulob*) although some of the outsider families had been residents of the peninsula since the 1600s. The outsiders had constrained the Maya on haciendas and had appropriated traditionally held community lands. The Maya aggressively organized to regain political autonomy in the Caste Wars. After the turn of the century and the Revolution of 1910, the Maya culture was well preserved in villages and *ranchos* along the frontier in the eastern territory of Quintana Roo. Quintana Roo became a state in 1974, and with the development of tourism on the east coast of the Yucatan peninsula, the political organization of life under the tropical canopy became formalized. Life in the village became more regulated, and as the Maya moved to confront the modern world, they diminished their ability to return to traditional lifeways in the forest. The forest was cut down, the population exploded, and the ancient pattern of life eroded.

To explain the unexplainable, the Maya populate their world with supernatural beings. On the ground, traditional *h-men*, Catholic priests, and Pentecostal ministers lead the people in rituals that petition the gods, the spirits, and supernatural forces. Offerings are made so that humans are protected. The communal act of participating in services binds the society more closely together, presents a collective stance toward the world, repeats and reinforces a world view, and legitimizes action with supernatural sanction.

The traditional practitioner of rites and rituals, the *h-men*, tried and usually succeeded in manipulating the natural world. By imitative magic that was thought to produce a desired effect merely by imitating the effect, the *h-men* produced rain, cleansed the town of evil winds, and buried the evil part of a child in the *K'ex* ceremony. With these actions, the *h-men* reduced anxiety and fear and solidified social ties. The traditional religious ceremonies performed by the Maya were reflections of their society. The ceremonies involved not only natural forces (symbols of the wind, thunder, rain, frogs, important plants, animals such as wild deer, *jabali*) but also the elders, their sons, their grandsons, and sometimes wives, daughters, and granddaughters, a perfect reflection of the social network.

Mayan religion offers a sense of stability to the people and a profound understanding of the way the world is organized. For the Maya, religion has been a powerful force from pre-Columbian times, and it has remained powerful in the modern era. The ancient pre-Columbian religion has contributed a series of supernatural beings that are mainly nature spirits who protect or plague the Maya in the forest (i.e., Sipiceh, the Owner of the Forest, Protector of Deer), in their *milpa* (*alux*, dwarf-tricksters; and *tun*, spirits in large stones), and in their dealings with bees or cattle (i.e., X-Juan-Thul).

The religion that has permeated the peninsula from the sixteenth century is Catholicism. Its main contribution to the modern Maya may be social. The worship of or attention on saints has brought groups of men together to participate in festivals focused on the welfare of the whole community. The new religion in Coba is Pentecostalism. Its contribution to the Maya has been to focus on the individual.

The H-men

The old man reflected on the past (Figure 7.3). "It was pure Catholic, pure yerbateros, *pure* h-men, *and there were not so many doctors. About fifty years ago, there were not so many religions. Now there are Catholics, Pentecostals, Evangelists, and more. They all go to their temples and adore God. But fifty to sixty years ago, there were only Catholics,* yerbateros, *and* h-men. *Then everyone in the world made* Chachac, Lolcatal, U-hanli-col, *and* U-hanli-cab *ceremonies. Nowadays, people have stopped making the traditional rites to guard themselves."*

The Milpero

The milpero *reflected on the present.* "The years are very dry now, much drier than in my father's time. The harvests fail, we can't harvest enough corn to feed us for a year. The rains are too light or too heavy, and our crops are lost. Finding someone to help cut the milpa *is hard. I paid two men from Chemax to assist me, and I never saw them again. They took my money, promised to help me, and never came back. I saw them one time in Chemax and asked them what*

Figure 7.3. The yerbatero *Jose Isabel Cocom.*

happened. They promised to come and help me, but the hardest work is done now. They came and cut down brush in my old milpa. *Now the size of my field is too small to feed my family for a year if we get a bad harvest. I'll go to the coast and work. I'll work building a hotel at Akumal. The pay is very low, but we need cash to buy corn."*

Nicolas would be forty years old this year and had worked as a milpero *all his life. He had cut* chicle, *worked construction on the Isla Mujeres to the north, and raised cattle. His wife Maria raised pigs and chickens and tended to her kitchen gardens. The family was large, twelve in all, Nicolas and Maria, five sons, and five daughters. Nicolas reflected on the future. He swung in his hammock out in his* milpa, *listening to the birds singing and hearing the bus or cars traveling to the east to Tulum. His oldest son, Pedro, was nearing the age to marry. His son Nicolas was helping him in the* milpa. *He looked forward to the time when he could work with all of his sons to make a* nohoch col (*a large* milpa). *With his sons working with him, he would prosper. He would hold ceremonies in the field to protect his family. The large size of his* milpa *would ensure that he could provide sufficient food for the members of his family* (Figure 7.4). *He looked at his wife, Maria, cutting up a watermelon. She handed him a piece and took one for herself. The melon was sweet, and they saved the seeds to plant again. He had worked to provide for his family, and the web of kinship would provide for him and his wife as they grew old.*

Figure 7.4. Nainal (storehouse) in the milpa of Nicolas Caamal Canche.

Figure 7.5. Children returning a soda bottle to the store.

The Children

It was late afternoon when Nicolas and Maria returned to the village. Nicolas had a load of corn he carried on his back by a tumpline crossing his forehead. Maria carried a load of wood for the hearth. As they entered town, they walked past the cemetery. A new tomb had been placed there for Silvestre May Balam, who represented the past as Nicolas and Maria represented the present. They saw their young son Jose Feliciano and their daughter Reina squatting by the side of their yard. The two children were chewing on small ears of corn, biting into the kernels, and in their other hand, they each held a bottle of Coke. These children represented the future (Figure 7.5).

Appendix A: Time Periods and Characters

THE CLASSIC PERIOD (A.D. 600–900)

Jaguar Paw, Curl Snout, and Stormy Sky—Rulers of Tikal

Pacal the Great, the Queen Zak-Kuk and Chan Bahlum, son of Pacal—Rulers of Palenque

Ix Chebel Yax—Patroness of Coba, Goddess Weaver, Creator Goddess, Mistress of the Earth, wife of Itzam Na

Itzam Na Kauil (usually just Itzam Na)—Rain God, "Iguana House Bountiful Harvest"

Sac Itzam Na—Uncle of *Itzam Na;* his color symbolizes north

Chac Itzam Na—Brother of Izam Na *Kauil*; his color symbolizes east

Ah Kin—The Diviner; a priest

Ah Nacom—The Sacrificer; a priest

THE EARLY POST-CLASSIC PERIOD (A.D. 900–1200)

Kinchil Coba—Ruler of ancient Coba, lord of Coba during the Itza hegemony

Itza—The foreign dynasty that ruled at Chichen Itza

THE LATE POST-CLASSIC PERIOD (A.D. 1283–1511)

Ah Paal Canul—Guardian of the wall of Mayapan and murderer of the Cocom ruler

Nachi Cocom—Son of the Cocom ruler of Mayapan who escaped the slaughter of his family and, after the collapse of Mayapan, traveled to Tibolon and Sotuta founding the Cocom capitals in the eastern province of Yucatan

Xiu dynasty—Enemies of the Cocom who had their capital at Mani in the western sector of Yucatan

THE CONTACT PERIOD AND THE CONQUEST (A.D. 1511–1547)

Ah Kin—Maya priest, "He of the Sun"

Bach Can—"Chachalaca Snake," a *milpero* at the time of contact with the Spaniards

Geronimo de Aguilar—A Spaniard who was shipwrecked off the eastern coast of Yucatan in 1511; he learned the native language and was picked up by Hernando Cortes in 1519, served as a translator, and accompanied Cortes during the conquest of Central Mexico

Gonzalo Guerrero—A Spaniard who was shipwrecked off the eastern coast of Yucatan in 1511; he took a native wife, became a great warrior among the Indians, and refused to rejoin the Spaniards who landed on the east coast in 1519

Francisco de Montejo the Father—Initiator of the first campaign to conquer Yucatan

Francisco de Montejo the Younger—The illegitimate son of Francisco de Montejo; initiator of the second and third campaigns to conquer Yucatan

Nacon Cupul—*Cacique* (ruler) of the village of Chichen Itza

Nacahun Noh—The powerful and feared war chief of Saci

Napot Xiu—The Xiu "Rain bringer" who on a pilgrimage to Chichen Itza in 1536 was murdered with his attendants in the settlement of Otzmal by the Cocom as an act of revenge

Montejo the Father's Nephew—Conqueror of the eastern provinces of Yucatan

Tamayo Pacheco—A Spaniard who put down the Indian rebellion in the year 1546

THE COLONIAL PERIOD (A.D. 1547–1812)

Lorenzo Cocom—Brother of Nachi Cocom; fierce ruler of the Cocom at Sotuta

Diego de Landa—Franciscan friar who entered the Yucatan in 1549

Lahun Canche—*Holpop* or head of the Canche lineage; resident of Kanxoc

Jacinto Canek—*Kan ek', lucero,* the morning star; leader of the Maya in the rebellion of 1761

THE REVOLUTIONARY PERIOD (A.D. 1812–1915)

Tomas May—A *tatiche* or follower of the Talking Cross who led the rebellion against the federal forces at Kanxoc

Francisco May—Resident of Kanxoc during the turbulant Caste War of Yucatan

Bonifacio May—Younger brother of Francisco May and a *campesino* at the Hacienda Yaxnic

Teodosio May—Older brother of Francisco May who lived in Tepich

Don Silvestre May—Son of Francisco May; resident of Kanxoc, and founder of the settlement at Coba

THE MODERN PERIOD (A.D. 1930–1987)

Don Demetrio Pol—*H-men* living at the rancho Chac Ne

Don Jose Isabel Cocom—*Yerbatero* living in the village of Coba

Don Panfilo Canche—Don Silvestre's son-in-law; one of the early settlers of Coba

Doña Juliano May—Don Silvestre's daughter; Don Panfilo's wife

Don Jose Maria Caamal Uh—Don Silvestre's *compadre;* one of the first settlers of Coba, Nicolas Caamal's father

Bernabel Cen—One of the early settlers of Coba from Tixhualatun; a *campesino* who located most of the *sacbeob* or ancient roads in Coba

Don Fernando Cen—One of the early settlers of Coba from Tixhualatun; the first mayor of Coba

Don Dolores Cen—One of the early settlers of Coba from Tixhualatun

Pedro Celesino Noh—Don Silvestre's son-in-law and one of the early settlers of Coba

Dona Emilia May—Don Silvestre's daughter; wife of Pedro Celestino Noh

Arturo Chimal—An early settler of Coba from Kanxoc

Don Silvino Uicab—An early settler of Coba from Kanxoc

Teodoro May—An early settler of Coba from Kanxoc

Daniel Cen—A beekeeper in Coba who made his fortune selling honey; a president of the Ejido of Coba

Don Lorenzo Itza—*Dueño* of the rancho San Raphael and store owner in Coba; one of the richest men in the village

Nicolas Caamal Canche—A *milpero;* the son of Jose Maria Caamal Uh

Florentino Cen—Sixth mayor of Coba

Elusio Cuyoc—Resident of Coba

Felipe Chan—Resident of Coba

Maria Pastora Vivas Oxtet—Wife of Nicolas Caamal Canche

Appendix B: Glossary of Yucatec, Spanish, and Anthropological Terms

abuelos: Grandparents
acalche: Wooded swamp
Acción de gracias: A ritual of thanksgiving to protect a family or a group from evil
    spirits
achiote: Bixa Orellana, a shrub or small tree whose seeds are used for coloring rice
    or as a dye, also used as a medicinal remedy
aqua potable: potable drinking water system
Ah Kin: ''He of the Sun''; a priest
Ah lelem caan chac: Chac with lightning
Ah Nacon: The sacrificer
Ahau: Lord, ruler
alamo: Ficus cotinifolia, one of the largest trees in the region, used for making a kind
    of paper
alux: Dwarf tricksters who are forest spirits; clay mask representing an alux, which
    had protective powers
anicab: Arrabidaea floribunda, a vine from the rainforest used to tie house poles to-
    gether, to tie thatch to roof poles, and as material for baskets
apiculture: Bee-keeping
apazote: Chenopodium ambrosioides, a medicinal herb
arboriculture: The systematic cultivation and harvest of trees and/or their products
arroz: Rice
artesanias: Handicraft stores that sell regional crafts
atole: Corn gruel beverage

Bacabs: Wind Gods and Sky Bearers
balam: Anthropomorphic spirits of the forest or pure air, they come as wind; also
    jaguar, a family name
balsamito: Plant used to treat dysentery
balche: Lonchocarpus longistylus, a tree whose bark is used to make ceremonial
    wine when mixed with honey or sugar and fermented
barrios: Wards or neighborhoods of a village or town
batab: Native term for governor
beans: *Phaseolus vulgaris*
bilateral cross-cousin marriage: A marriage in which a male seeks a wife from the set
    of his father's sister's daughters or his mother's brother's daughters
bilimcoc: Plant used as a remedy for asthma
blancos: White men
bobtun: Leaves tied around a central pole in the Los Corrales ceremony
Box luum: Rich, fertile black soil
burro: A wooden frame used by the Catholic Church during the Inquisition to torture
    natives who had fallen away from the ''true faith''
butun: A limestone outcrop
buul: Phaseolus vulgaris; beans
buyluum: A plant that grows only during the rainy season

caanche: A raised kitchen garden or a small carved cedar bench

cacao: Theobroma cacao: chocolate beans from the cacao tree

cacicazgo: Native Maya kingdom

cacique: Native Maya ruler or lord

calabaza: Squash

campesino: Rural farmer

Cañada: Secondary growth in an abandoned *milpa*

casita: A small hut in the *milpa*

cedar: *Cedrela mexicana,* the wood of which is light, coarse, and soft, with a distinctive odor, valued for its use in furniture, doors, rafters, and general construction

celantro: Coriander sativum, an herb used to flavor food

cenote: Limestone sinkhole, usually holding water

Cenote Sagrado: The Sacred Cenote at Chichen Itza, an entrance into the Maya Underworld where idols and humans were sacrificed

Chac: The Rain God

chacah: Bursera Simaruba, a tree with medicinal qualities

chacal-haaz: The fruit of the mamey tree

Chachac: Traditional rain ceremony performed by the *h-men* and community members

chache: A pole rack placed over a fire to dry fresh meat

chac luum: Red soil

chacmolche: *Erythrina americana,* a small, spiny tree that produces poisonous seeds

Chac Ne: The rancho of Don Demetrio Pol, sole practicing *h-men* in Coba

Chacob: The mighty Rain Gods, the rain-bringers

chakan: *Xtabai* in the form of a green and yellow snake

ch'amac: Foxes or lynxes; beasts of prey

chan cuento: A small bill run up in a store, a debt

chapak: Weeds found on lake shores used to treat skin diseases

chaya: Jatropha aconitifolia, a small tree whose leaves are edible

chechem: *Metropium Brownei,* the "black poison-wood" tree

chi'bal: Term for the lineage group of the male

chicle: Gum sap from the *zapote* tree *(Achras zapote)*

chiclero: A man who cuts the *zapote* tree deep in the forest to extract *chicle* or gum resin; a seasonal worker

Chilam Balam: Jaguar Speaker, the Jaguar Prophet of the ancient Maya

chile del monte: Capsium frutescens, wild chile

chile habanero: Capsium sp., small, green, hot chile peppers, domesticated and grown in kitchen gardens

chol pakal: Garden

chu: Gourds used as water jugs by the Maya

chuyche: Pole-and-thatch house

cimi: A day name in the Maya calendar, "death"

coa: A small curved knife used to cut weeds

Cobaeños: People of Coba

coc: Asthma

col: Milpa or cornfield

colecab: The stingless honeybees of Yucatan

cololche: Woven sapling fences

comadres: Ritual ties between natural mothers and female godparents

comal: A griddle placed over three hearth stones, used to make tortillas

compadrazgo: The system of godparenthood introduced by the Spaniards and modified by the Maya to suit their own needs

compadres: Ritual tie between a natural father and male godparent

CONASUPO: Compañia Nacional de Subsistencias Populares, a store that sells basic food products and other goods at below private retail prices to lower-income families through federally operated outlets

Copal: Protium copal; pom, incense

COPLAMAR: Comisión de Planeación para Zonas Marginados, the Commission for Planning in Marginal Zones; in Coba the sponsoring agency for a massive reforestation project employing local people

copo: Ficus cotinifolia, the *alamo* tree whose bark was pounded to make paper

creoles: People born in New Spain of strict Spanish descent

cross-cousin: The mother's brother's children or the father's sister's children, acceptable marriage partners in unilineal systems of kinship

Cruzob: The *Tatichos,* Indians of the eastern sector of the peninsula the most traditional Maya and never controlled by the state or national governments; independent Maya and followers of the Talking Cross

cumche: Pileus mexicanus, a tree whose fruits are edible

cup: Calopogonium coeruleum, a kind of wild jicama, a root eaten in time of famine

doctrina: Catechisms of the Roman Catholic Church

delegado: Mayor

dueño: Owner

dzulob: Foreigners (dzul: foreigner)

ejidarios: Members of an *ejido,* communal land-holding organization granted by the federal government as a result of the 1910 Revolution reforms

ejido: A communal land grant issued to rural farmers by the federal government

Ek Chuah: The ancient Maya God of Merchants

elote: Corn

encomenderos: Spanish landowners of the Colonial period; "entrusted ones"

encomienda: A system in which groups of Indians were indentured to the Spanish conquistadors and other early settlers; the Indians were required to pay the foreigners tribute

entrada: An entrance or an invasion

estancias: Spanish cattle ranches established in the Colonial period

extended family: A family consisting of three generations, a man and woman, their children, and grandchildren or a family consisting of brothers, their wives, and children

fagina: Communal labor for the welfare of the whole community; a labor draft called by the mayor

federales: The Mexican national police force

gordas: Thick tortillas frequently taken to eat cold in the *milpa*

guano: Inodes japa, a large-leafed palm used as thatch for the roof of a house, for mats, or for making brooms

Guardia Nacional: The National Guard

haancab: Bride service in which the groom serves temporarily in enhancing the economic activities of his father-in-law

habin: *Piscidia communis,* a tree, the leaves of which are used on the altar of the Chachac ceremony

hacendado: Hacienda or plantation owner

hacienda: A plantation where Indians labored as virtual slaves attached to the land by debt peonage

halach uinic: "True Man," the ruler or headman

henequen: *Agave fourcroydes,* a source of fiber

Hetzmek: A ceremony to celebrate the first time a baby is seated on the mother's hip rather than cradled in her arms

h-men: Traditional Maya priest-curer; a shaman

holpop: The head of a lineage group

hool: *Hampea trilobata,* a large shrub or small tree whose bark contains strong fiber and is used for tying

hubnak: Diarrhea

huipil: Traditional Maya woman's dress

ik: Spirits that appear as winds

ikim: An individual who exhibits "doubles"; for example, double teeth, one behind the other, double whorls of hair on the head, and who is said to grind his or her teeth and "devour" younger siblings or the mother of the child, causing illness or death within the family

itz: Zapote resin

Itza: The ruling family of Chichen Itza, "Water Witch"

Itzam Na: "Iguana House," Creator God, Rain God, "He Who Dwelt in the Sky"

Ix Chebel Yax: "Lady Unique of the Painted Brushes," "Lady Unique Owner of the Cloth," Goddess Weaver, Creator Goddess, Mistress of Earth, Rain Goddess, wife of *Itzam Na*

Ixmoja: *Nohoch Mul* or the large mound, a pyramid structure at Coba

jabali: Wild pig

jicara: *Crescentia Cujete,* gourd cups used for offerings in the *Chachac* and other ceremonies

jornalero de campo: A field worker

Juan del Monte: *Dueño* or owner of the forest; guardian of the forest, and the owner of *chicle*

kancab: Red earth mortar

Kan ek': *Lucero,* the morning star, Venus

k'an luum: Yellow soil

karst: A type of topography formed on limestone with sinkholes, caves and underground drainage

katun: 7,200 days in the Maya calendrical round; a time span used for seating rulers at particular Maya settlements

K'ex: A traditional ritual performed to transform an *ikim* to a "normal" state of being

Kin: The sun, a day

Kinich Ahau: The Sun God

Kukulcan: The "Feathered Serpent," priest-ruler of Chichen Itza

lateritic soil formation: The process of hardpan formation due to the baking action of the sun

leaching: The process of nutrient depletion in soils due to the washing action of torrential rains

lec: *Lagenaria siceraria,* a round gourd used as a cup

lelem: A wooden sword used in the *Chachac* ceremony symbolizing lightning

leña: Firewood

limosnas: Alms required by the Roman Catholic Church during the Colonial period.

Lolcatali: A traditional ritual performed to protect a houselot or a village from evil spirits

Los Corrales: A traditional ceremony held to guard cattle and the family that owns them

Macal: Dioscorea alata L., cultivated for its edible root
machete: A large heavy metal knife used for cutting underbrush by the Maya
Maize: *Zea mays,* corn, the staff of life
mal ojo: Evil eye
mal viento: Evil winds that strike a person and cause debilitation, sickness, or death
manta: Cotton cloth
marquetas: Blocks of boiled *chicle* gum resin
masa: Corn dough
metate: Stone slab on which corn is ground
milpa: The cornfield, in which beans, squash, and other vegetables are also grown
milpero: The corn farmer
moan: Mythical bird associated with death
molinero: Corn miller
molino: Corn grinder (hand or motor driven)
monte: The forest
monte alto: High rainforest
monte bajo: Low rainforest; scrub forest
municipio: Municipality
musencabob: Supernatural bees believed to reside at Coba

Naab: Nymphaea ampla, the water lily found in lake zones and an important symbol
in ancient Maya iconography
naal name: The wife's kinship group
nacom: A war leader
nainal: Corn storehouse usually located in the *milpa*
nal: Zea mays, a fast ripening variety of corn usually planted in small fields adjacent
to the house
naranja agria: Sour orange tree; *zutspakal*
Nicte: A cult of debauchery; "flor de Mayo" (a flower of Maya), *Plumeria*
nohoch col: Larger than average cornfield
nohoch tata: "Great Father," esteemed elder
nohua: Large, thick ceremonial tortillas
novia: Girlfriend
nuclear family: A man, woman, and their offspring

obvenciones: Head taxes under the colonial government
on: Avocado
oracones: The upright tree trunks that serve as support posts in a house
oratorio: A small household shrine

panuchos: Tortillas stuffed with black beans and topped with tomatoes, onion, egg,
and chile
patron: A wealthy owner of a hacienda or any wealthy, important man
pepita: Squash seed
petate: A woven rush mat
peten: A flat plate woven of the *anicab* vine, hung from the rafters, it is used to store
food and to protect it from rats
pib: An earthen oven
pich: Enterolobium cyclocarpum, a tree whose fruit can be used to make bread
pila: A trough that holds liquid
Plumeria: *Nicte,* "flor de Mayo" (a flower of May)
pom: Protium copal, a tree that produces a resin used as incense; incense
popolna: The men's house
pozole: A type of maize gruel beverage

presidente del ejido: The President of the *ejido* or communal land grant
principal: An important man
pueblo: Village
put: Carica papaya; the papaya tree
putz luum: Dry soil without stones

quincunx: Four dots in a square with another dot in the center; a symbol of the Maya world
Quiebrahacha: *Krugiodendron ferreum,* a hard wood of Yucatan, axe-master

ramon: Brosium alicastrum, a tall tree whose leaves are used as cattle feed; the nut of the *ramon* was used by the Maya as famine food
rebozo: Traditional shawl
reciprocal exchange: Direct exchange of goods and/or labor among family members and/or friends
redistribution: Centralization of goods and reallocation to adapt to ecological constraints and possibilities
relleno negro: Maya stew
repartimiento: A colonial system to extract exportable goods and labor from Indian subjects

saca: Maize gruel used as an offering in traditional ceremonies
sacate: Pasture grass used in the Los Corrales ceremony
sacbe: Ancient Maya road
sas: A crystal that the *h-men* use to see into the past or into the future
sascab: Granular limestone used as plaster
sascabera: Ancient mines (open and capped) where granular limestone was extracted to be used as lime plaster
Savanna: Grasslands
Scroll Baby emblem: A mark of a royal kin group
segundos: Seconds or alternatives to medicinal plants in a curing remedy
sip: Spirits that are associated with different plants
sipiceh: King of the deer, a spirit of the forest that guards the animals
solar: Yard area adjacent to the house, usually surrounded by a stone wall or barbed wire fence
sop: Brush fence constructed around the *milpa*
Squash: *Cucurbita moschata*
Stela: An ancient inscribed stone monument
subin: Acacia globifera, a tree covered with thorns and biting red ants

tancazche: Zanthoxylum pagara, a tree whose roots are masticated as a local anesthesia for toothache
Tancazik: Evil wind
Tata Naz: Interpreter or "Speaker for the Talking Cross"
Tatich: "Patron of the Talking Cross"
tepescuintli: Small rodent of the tropical rainforest
tok: Obsidian flake, bladelet used in bloodletting
tortillas: Corn pancakes
tumpline: A woven strap set across the forehead and tied to loads on the back; used to transport heavy loads
tun (tunob): Spirit(s) that reside(s) in large stones; also the 360-day cycle in the Maya calendar
tunkel: Wooden drum used by the Maya in ceremonies
Tupp-kak: A traditional ceremony performed by the *h-men* to make the ground cool again after the flames have burned brush in a new milpa

uaay: Animal spirits of evil sorcerers

U-hanli-cab: A traditional ritual to protect wild bee colonies and the family that has them

U-hanli-col: A traditional ritual performed to protect the *milpa* and the family that works it

uinal: A period of 20 days

u kaxiltabal kik: Severe bloody diarrhea

u kin pek: "The dog days," the *canicula,* the *veranillo,* the rainless days during the rainy season

unilineal descent system: Membership in a kinship group that is exclusively recognized through either the father's or the mother's kinship line

X Balam Na: Jaguar House, Church of the Talking Cross

xcambalhau: Dorstenia Contrajerva, an antidote for every poison including snakebite

xickanic: "I am going."

ximche: Casearia pitida, the maize tree, which bears a fruit that resembles maize; used to construct arches across the ceremonial table in the *Chachac* ceremony

Xix Ek: "Wasp Star" or Venus Cult

X-Juan-Thul: The spirit who lives in the cattle corral

Xtabai: The sorceress, a beautiful woman whose touch is ice cold and whose embrace results in death or madness

xul: Digging stick; also the name of a month in the Maya "finished" calendar

ya, zac-ya: The *zapote* tree that gives *chicle*

Yaxche: The first tree, the *ceiba* at the center of the world

yerbatero: Herbal curer

yerbabuena: Mentha citrata, a highly aromatic herb useful as tea or as a condiment

Yum Cimil: Lord of Death

Zapote: Achras zapote, a tree that supplies *chicle* (gum resin) during the rainy season

Zutspakal: Naranja agria, sour orange

References

Abrams, Elliot M. 1987 "Economic Specialization and Construction Personnel in Classic Period Copan, Honduras." *American Antiquity* 52(3):485–499.

Adams, R.E.W. 1970 "Suggested Classic Period Occupational Specialization in the Southern Maya Lowlands." *Papers of the Peabody Museum of Archaeology and Ethnology* 61:437–502

Aguirre Beltran, G. 1979 *Regions of Refuge*. Washington, DC: Society for Applied Anthropology, Monograph 12.

Anderson, Edgar. 1952 *Plants, Man and Life*. Berkeley: University of California.

Andrews, Anthony and Fernando Robles C. 1985 "Chichen Itza and Coba: An Itza-Maya Standoff in Early Postclassic Yucatan." In *The Lowland Maya Postclassic*. Arlen F. Chase and P. M. Rice, eds. Austin: University of Texas Press, pp. 62–72.

Baklanoff, Eric N. 1980 "The Diversification Quest: A Monocrop Export Economy in Transition." In *Yucatan: A World Apart*. Edward H. Moseley and Edward D. Terry, eds. Birmingham: The University of Alabama Press, pp. 202–244.

Barrera Marin, Alfredo, Alfredo Barrera Vazquez and Rosa Maria Lopez Franco. 1976 *Nomenclatura Etnobotanica Maya*. Mexico: Instituto Nacional de Antropologia e Historia.

Beals, Ralph L. 1975 *The Peasant Marketing System of Oaxaca, Mexico*. Berkeley: University of California Press.

Becker, Marshall. 1973 "Archaeological Evidence for Occupational Specialization Among the Classic Period Maya at Tikal, Guatemala." *American Antiquity* 38:396–406.

Brand, D.D. 1951 *Quiroga, a Mexican Municipio*. Washington, DC: Smithsonian Institution Institute of Social Anthropology, Publication 11.

Bricker, Victoria R. 1981 *The Indian Christ, the Indian King*. Austin: University of Texas Press.

Chamberlain, Robert. 1966 *The Conquest and Colonialization of Yucatan: 1517–1550*. New York: Octagon Books, Inc.

Coe, Michael. 1978 *Lords of the Underworld*. Princeton: Princeton University Press.

Cook, Scott and Martin Diskin, 1976 *Markets in Oaxaca*. Austin: University of Texas Press.

Edmunson, Munro S. 1982 *The Ancient Future of the Itza: The Book of Chilam Balam of Tizimin*. Austin: University of Texas Press.

Eggan, Fred. 1934 "The Maya Kinship System and Cross-cousin Marriage." *American Anthropologist* 36:188–202.

Farriss, Nancy. 1984 *Maya Colonial Society Under Colonial Rule*. Princeton: Princeton University Press.

Folan, William, Laraine A. Fletcher and Ellen R. Kintz 1979 "Fruit, Fiber, Bark and Resin: The Social Organization of a Maya Urban Center." *Science* 204:697–701.

Folan, William, Laraine A. Fletcher and Ellen R. Kintz. 1983 *Coba: A Classic Maya Metropolis*. New York: Academic Press.

Harris, David R. 1972 "Swidden Systems and Settlement." In *Man, Settlement and Urbanism*. Peter J. Ucko, Ruth Tringham and G.W. Dimbleby, eds. London: Duckworth, pp. 245–262.

Hester, J.A. 1954 *Maya Agriculture*. Washington, DC: Carnegie Institution of Washington Yearbook, 53 (1953–1954):297–298.

Kearney Michael. 1972 *The Winds of Ixtepeji: World View and Society in a Zepotec Town*. New York: Holt, Rinehart and Winston, Inc.

Kelly, I. and A. Palerm. 1952 *The Tajin Totonac. Part 1: History, Subsistence, Shelter and Technology*. Washington, DC: Smithsonian Institution, Institute of Social Anthropology, Publication 13.

Kintz, Ellen. 1983 "Cottage Industry and Guild Formation in a Classic Maya Metropolis." In *Coba: A Classic Maya Metropolis*. William Folan, Ellen R. Kintz and Laraine A. Fletcher, eds. New York: Academic Press, pp. 149–159.

Levi-Strauss, Claude. 1962 *The Savage Mind*. Chicago: The University of Chicago Press.

Lundell, C.L. 1937 *The Vegetation of the Peten*. Washington, DC: Carnegie Institution of Washington, Publication 478.

Marcus, Joyce. 1982 "The Plant World of the Sixteenth- and Seventeenth-Century Lowland Maya." In *Maya Subsistence*. Kent Flannery, ed. New York: Academic Press, pp. 239–273.

McBride, F.W. 1947 *Cultural and Historical Geography of Southwest Guatemala*. Washington, DC: Smithsonian Institution, Institute of Social Anthropology, Publication 4.

Montes de Oca, Rosa Elena. 1977 "The State and Peasants." In *Authoritarianism in Mexico*. J.L. Reyna and R.S. Weinert, eds. Philadelphia: Institute for the Study of Human Issues, Inc, pp. 47–63.

Muñoz, Hernaldo, ed. 1981 *From Dependency to Development: Strategies to Overcome Underdevelopment and Inequality*. Boulder: Westview Press.

Nelson, Michael. 1973 *The Development of Tropical Lands: Policy Issues in Latin America*. Baltimore: Johns Hopkins University Press.

Nutini, Hugo G. 1984 *Ritual Kinship*. Princeton: Princeton University Press.

Pohl, Mary and Lawrence H. Feldman. 1982 "The Traditional Role of Women and Animals in Lowland Maya Economy." In *Maya Subsistence*. Kent Flannery, ed. New York: Academic Press, pp. 295–311.

Pollock, H.E.D., R. Roys, T. Proskouriakoff and A.L. Smith. 1962 *Mayapan, Yucatan, Mexico*. Washington, DC: Carnegie Institution of Washington, Publication 619.

Redfield, R. and A. Villa Rojas. 1934 *Chan Kom, A Maya Village*. Washington, DC: Carnegie Institute of Washington, Publication 448.

Reed, Nelson. 1964 *The Caste War of Yucatan*. Stanford: Stanford University Press.

Robicsek, Francis and D.E. Hales. 1981 *The Maya Book of the Dead: The Ceramic Codex*. Charlotteville: University of Virginia Art Museum.

Roys, Ralph. 1931 *The Ethnobotany of the Maya*. New Orleans: Tulane University of Louisiana Middle American Research Series, 2.

Roys, Ralph. 1957 *The Political Geography of the Yucatan Maya*. Washington, DC: Carnegie Institution of Washington, Publication 613.

Roys, Ralph. 1962 "Literary Sources for the History of Mayapan." In *Mayapan, Yucatan, Mexico*. H.E.D. Pollock, Ralph Roys, T. Proskouriakoff and A. Ledyard Smith, eds. Washington, DC: Carnegie Institution of Washington, Publication 619, pp. 25–86.

Roys, Ralph. 1965 *Ritual of the Bacabs*. Norman: University of Oklahoma Press.

Roys, Ralph. 1967 *The Book of Chilam Balam of Chumayel*. Norman: University of Oklahoma.

Sanders, William. 1973 "The Cultural Ecology of the Lowland Maya: A Reevaluation." In *The Classic Maya Collapse*. T. Patrick Culbert, ed. Albuquerque: University of New Mexico Press, pp. 325–365.

Schele, L. and M.E. Miller. 1986 *The Blood of Kings: Dynasty and Ritual in Maya Art*. New York: George Brazieller, Inc.

Simpson, Eyler N. 1937 *The Ejido: Mexico's Way Out*. Chapel Hill: The University of North Carolina Press.

Smith, C. Earle Jr. and Marguerita L. Cameron. 1977 "Ethnobotany of the Puuc, Yucatan." *Economic Botany* 31:93–110.

Standley, Paul C. 1930 *Flora of the Yucatan*. Chicago: Field Museum of Natural History Publication 279, Botanical Series 3(3).

Thompson, J.E.S. 1970 *Maya History and Religion*. Norman: University of Oklahoma Press.

Thompson, J.E.S., H.E.D. Pollock and J. Charlot. 1932 *A Preliminary Study of the Ruins of Coba, Quintana Roo, Mexico*. Washington, DC: Carnegie Institution of Washington, Publication 424.

Thompson, Richard A. 1974 *The Winds of Tomorrow*. Chicago: The University of Chicago Press.

Tozzer, A.L. (ed. and trans.) 1941 *Landa's Relacion de las Cosas de Yucatan*. Cambridge: Papers, Peabody Museum of American Archaeology and Ethnology, Harvard University, Vol. 18.

Turner, Victor. 1967 *The Forest of Symbols: Aspects of Ndembu Ritual*. Ithaca: Cornell University Press.

Upham, Steadman. 1982 *Politics and Power: An Economic and Political History of the Western Pueblo*. New York: Academic Press.

Villa Rojas, A. 1945 *The Maya of East Central Quintana Roo*. Washington, DC: Carnegie Institute of Washington, Publication 559.

Vivo Escoto, Jorge A. 1964 "Weather and Climate of Mexico and Central America." In *Handbook of Middle American Indians*, vol. 1. Robert West, volume ed. Austin: University of Texas Press, pp. 187–215.

Webster, D. 1985 "Surplus, Labor and Stress in Late Classic Maya Society." *Journal of Anthropological Research* 41(4):375–399.

Wells, Alan. 1985 *Yucatan's Guilded Age*. Albuquerque: University of New Mexico Press.

West, R.C. 1948 *Cultural Geography of the Modern Tarascan Area*. Washington, DC: Smithsonian Institution, Institute of Social Anthropology, Publication 7.

Wilson, Eugene. 1980 "Physical Geography of the Yucatan Peninsula." In *Yucatan. A World Apart*. E.H. Moseley and E.D. Terry, eds. Birmingham: University of Alabama Press, pp. 5–40.

Wisdom, C. 1940 *The Chorti Indians of Guatemala*. Chicago: University of Chicago Press.

Index

The passages in the book that are printed in italic type are contemporary personal stories, folk tales, myths, historical reconstructions, etc., and were therefore not read for indexing.

Page numbers in italic type below indicate a map or an illustration.